UNSHACKLING HUMANITY

HUMAN RIGHTS IN AFRICA AND THE GENESIS OF THE UDHR

KIZITO AKEJE

Copyright 2023 © **Kizito Akeje**

For more Inquiries contact
Email: kizitoakeje38@gmail.com
Phone number: +2349029523460

ISBN: 9798854248853

Preface

In a world that has witnessed the resilience of the human spirit amid countless challenges, the struggle for human rights stands as an indomitable force. It is with both reverence and urgency that I present "Unshackling Humanity: Human Rights in Africa and the Genesis of the UDHR." The African continent has been a crucible of human rights movements, a place where diverse cultures have embraced the innate dignity of every individual. From the ancient wisdom of pre-colonial societies to the fervor of independence struggles, Africa's journey towards justice and equality has been profound and complex.

At the heart of this transformative journey lies the Universal Declaration of Human Rights (UDHR), an iconic milestone in the quest for global human rights standards. This book delves deep into the historical context of human rights in Africa, exploring how the continent's rich tapestry of traditions and struggles contributed to shaping the very essence of the UDHR.As we traverse through time, we will witness the remarkable visionaries and leaders who dared to champion human rights amid oppression, violence, and inequality.

Their unwavering commitment to securing fundamental rights and freedoms serves as an eternal beacon of hope, illuminating our path towards a just and inclusive future. The decision to adopt the UDHR as a Declaration, rather than a treaty, was not merely a matter of semantics.

It reflected the need to enshrine a universal moral code that transcends the boundaries of legal obligations. Eleanor Roosevelt's passionate advocacy and the collective wisdom of the drafting committee elevated the Declaration to an emblem of shared humanity.

This book does not shy away from confronting the sobering realities of post-colonial Africa. As newfound nations grappled with nation-building, they encountered profound human rights challenges, from apartheid's brutal grip in South Africa to the agonizing tragedy of Rwanda's genocide.

The stories of resilience and resistance in the face of adversity serve as poignant reminders of the work that lies ahead. As we journey together, we will also explore the role of the International Criminal Court (ICC) in addressing human rights violations in Africa. This court, born out of the pursuit of justice, navigates treacherous waters as it seeks to hold perpetrators accountable while safeguarding human rights for all.

"Unshackling Humanity" also reflects on the strides made in promoting human rights, celebrating the triumphs and acknowledging the daunting road that stretches ahead. It is a testament to the indomitable human spirit and an invitation to build a future where human rights are cherished and protected in every corner of the world.

In conclusion, I hope that this book not only serves as an informative narrative but also ignites a collective call to action. Let us honor the legacy of those who fought for human rights and remain committed to uplifting humanity through our words, deeds, and unwavering determination.

With humility and hope,

Kizito

Contents

CHAPTER ONE

Introduction

In the annals of history, the struggle for human rights has been a resolute quest to uphold the inherent dignity and equality of every individual. As we embark on the journey of "Unshackling Humanity: Human Rights in Africa and the Genesis of the UDHR," we delve into the fascinating tapestry of Africa's history, where the fight for justice has woven itself into the fabric of countless societies. The African continent is a land of vibrant cultures, ancient traditions, and awe-inspiring resilience. From the majestic landscapes to the diverse communities that call it home, Africa has long been a cradle of civilization and a bastion of human potential. Yet, like any region, it has faced its share of trials, upheavals, and transformative moments that have shaped its human rights trajectory.

This book sets out to explore the historical context of human rights in Africa, tracing its roots from pre-colonial societies, where traditional systems of justice prevailed, to the tumultuous era of European colonization that left an indelible mark on the continent. Through the lens of Africa's struggle for independence and national sovereignty, we witness the emergence of visionary leaders who ignited the flame of human rights in their quest for freedom. At the core of our narrative stands the Universal Declaration of Human Rights (UDHR), a seminal document adopted by the United Nations General Assembly on December 10, 1948. With its 30 articles, the UDHR laid the foundation for a global framework of rights and freedoms, echoing the ancient wisdom of Africa's own traditions that revered the sanctity of life and the equality of all beings.

We will delve into the momentous journey that led to the adoption of the UDHR, exploring the contributions of African delegates and the international community in shaping this landmark declaration. The decision to embrace the UDHR as a Declaration, rather than a treaty, reflected a profound commitment to a universal moral code that transcends legal obligations—a declaration that speaks to the essence of shared humanity. The UDHR did not merely remain a distant ideal but seeped into the fabric of nations. Throughout this book, we will witness how African countries directly cited the principles of the UDHR in their municipal constitutions, infusing its spirit into their domestic legal systems. In doing so, they further reinforced the enduring relevance and impact of this historic document on the African continent.

Yet, the quest for human rights has been far from linear, and Africa, like any region, has faced its share of challenges and setbacks. Post-colonial independence struggles presented new hurdles as nations grappled with forging their identities and addressing systemic issues of discrimination and inequality. Our exploration will delve into pivotal moments of history, including the harrowing tragedies of apartheid in South Africa and the heart-wrenching genocide in Rwanda, reminding us of the gravity of human rights violations that must be confronted.

We will also navigate the realm of the International Criminal Court (ICC), established to hold perpetrators of gross human rights violations accountable for their actions. The ICC's mandate in addressing human rights violations in Africa has sparked debates and garnered international attention, leading us to examine the complexities and dilemmas faced in the pursuit of justice.

Amidst the challenges, this book will celebrate the triumphs and advancements made in the realm of human rights. Stories of resilience, the tireless efforts of civil society, NGOs, and grassroots movements, and the hope they instill will serve as a beacon of inspiration for the future.

In the grand tapestry of "Unshackling Humanity," we invite readers to join us on this odyssey of history, human rights, and the transformative power of advocacy. As we turn the pages, may we be reminded of the collective responsibility we share in uplifting humanity, respecting the sanctity of life, and safeguarding the precious rights of all individuals, regardless of race, creed, or nationality.

Fig 1: Protest against police brutality in Nigeria
Source: Kingsley Adrian, February 13, 2022

Meaning of Human Rights

The meaning of human rights is rooted in the principles of moral and ethical standards that define the fundamental rights and freedoms to which all individuals are inherently entitled simply by virtue of being human.

These rights are considered universal, inalienable, and egalitarian, applying to every person regardless of their age, ethnicity, location, religion, or any other status. Human rights are recognized and protected by both municipal (domestic) and international law.

Being inalienable means that human rights cannot be taken away or denied to individuals under any circumstances. They are considered inherent in all human beings, and no one should be deprived of these rights unjustly. These rights are applicable everywhere and at all times, transcending geographical and cultural boundaries. Human rights encompass a wide range of principles and norms, including but not limited to the right to life, liberty, and security; freedom from torture, slavery, and discrimination; the right to education, healthcare, and a standard of living adequate for one's well-being; and the right to freedom of thought, expression, and religion (Burns, 2014).

The concept of human rights emphasizes the importance of empathy, respect for others, and the rule of law. This means that individuals and governments have an obligation to uphold and protect the human rights of all people, respecting their dignity and ensuring that their rights are not violated. Human rights form the basis for promoting social justice, equality, and human dignity, fostering a society where every person can live with dignity and without fear of oppression or discrimination (James, etal 2013).

Overview of the importance of human rights in Africa

In cases where there may be legitimate reasons to limit or restrict certain rights, it is generally accepted that such actions should only be carried out through due process, with fair and transparent procedures based on specific circumstances and international legal standards.

Overall, human rights are a crucial pillar of the global community's efforts to create a world that upholds the values of justice, equality, and humanity.

The recognition and protection of human rights are essential for building a more peaceful, inclusive, and sustainable world where all individuals can flourish and reach their full potential.

The importance of human rights in Africa cannot be overstated, as they form the cornerstone of a just, equitable, and inclusive society. Human rights are fundamental rights and freedoms inherent to all individuals, regardless of race, ethnicity, gender, religion, or any other characteristic. They are grounded in the inherent dignity of every human being and are universally recognized and protected.

Throughout Africa's history, the struggle for human rights has been deeply intertwined with the continent's journey of liberation, self-determination, and nation-building. Here are some key aspects that highlight the significance of human rights in Africa:

1. Historical Context: Africa has a rich history of diverse cultures and civilizations, many of which upheld principles of justice, fairness, and respect for human dignity. However, the advent of European colonization in the 19th and 20th centuries imposed oppressive systems that violated the rights of Africans, leading to the need for a renewed commitment to human rights during the decolonization era.

2. Independence Struggles: The fight for human rights became an integral part of Africa's quest for independence from colonial rule. Visionary leaders,

activists, and grassroots movements united in demanding self-determination and equal rights for all Africans. This struggle against oppression became a catalyst for the acknowledgment and protection of human rights in newly independent nations.

3. Addressing Inequality: Africa, like any region, faces challenges related to economic disparity, social injustice, and discrimination. The promotion and protection of human rights are essential in addressing these disparities, uplifting marginalized communities, and ensuring equal opportunities for all.

4. Conflict and Violence: Many African nations have faced internal conflicts, civil wars, and instances of mass violence. Human rights play a vital role in seeking justice, accountability, and reconciliation in the aftermath of such events. Upholding human rights principles can contribute to conflict resolution and the prevention of further atrocities.

5. Empowerment of Marginalized Groups: Human rights are especially crucial in advancing the rights of vulnerable populations, including women, children, ethnic minorities, refugees, and persons with disabilities. Ensuring their rights are protected empowers them to participate fully in society and contribute to the region's development.

6. Strengthening Governance and Rule of Law: Respect for human rights is closely linked to good governance and the rule of law. Effective institutions that uphold human rights are essential for maintaining stability, fostering trust between governments and citizens, and promoting sustainable development.

7. Regional and International Cooperation: Human rights in Africa are not limited to national boundaries. The continent has seen significant engagement in regional human rights mechanisms, such as the African Charter

on Human and Peoples' Rights, as well as participation in global human rights conventions and treaties. International solidarity and cooperation are vital in addressing cross-border issues and ensuring accountability for human rights violations.

8. Sustainable Development: Human rights and sustainable development are interconnected. Ensuring access to basic necessities such as education, healthcare, and clean water, among others, is essential for human dignity and achieving sustainable development goals.

In conclusion, human rights in Africa are an indispensable foundation for a prosperous, just, and harmonious society. Acknowledging, promoting, and protecting human rights are not only ethical imperatives but also essential for achieving lasting peace, stability, and prosperity across the continent. The collective commitment to upholding human rights is a powerful force that can shape a brighter future for all Africans.

Background on the Universal Declaration of Human Rights (UDHR)

The Universal Declaration of Human Rights (UDHR) is a pivotal document in the realm of international human rights law. It was adopted by the United Nations General Assembly on December 10, 1948, as a response to the atrocities and suffering witnessed during World War II. The formation of the United Nations (UN) after the war provided an opportune platform to establish a global framework for safeguarding and promoting human rights. The drafting of the UDHR involved collaboration among representatives from various countries, human rights experts, and non-governmental organizations. Led by Eleanor Roosevelt, the drafting committee worked diligently to articulate a comprehensive set of human rights principles, guided by the UN Charter's commitment to the dignity and worth of every individual.

The UDHR comprises a preamble and 30 articles, outlining a broad range of civil, political, economic, social, and cultural rights. These rights are considered fundamental to the well-being and dignity of all human beings.

They include the right to life, liberty, and security; freedom of thought, conscience, and religion; freedom from torture, slavery, and discrimination; and the right to education, healthcare, and work. Although the UDHR is not legally binding, its moral and political significance is profound.

It serves as a shared aspiration for all nations and peoples, inspiring efforts to protect and uphold human rights globally. The principles articulated in the UDHR have influenced the development of subsequent human rights treaties and conventions, providing the groundwork for modern international human rights law. The Universal Declaration of Human Rights stands as a poignant reflection of humanity's collective commitment to recognizing and respecting the inherent dignity and rights of every individual. It remains an enduring symbol of our aspiration for a world founded on principles of equality, justice, and solidarity.

The concept of human rights has had a profound impact on the field of international law and has influenced the operations of global and regional institutions. States and non-governmental organizations play a crucial role in shaping public policy worldwide based on the principles of human rights. In times of peace, the idea of human rights serves as a common moral language that transcends borders and cultures.

Women delegates from various countries played a key role in getting women's rights included in the Declaration.
Hansa Mehta of India (standing above Eleanor Roosevelt) is widely credited with changing the phrase "All men are born free and equal" to "All human beings are born free and equal" in Article 1 of the Universal Declaration of Human Rights.
Source: New York, May 1946. UN Photo

Despite its significant influence, the doctrine of human rights has been met with skepticism and ongoing debates regarding its content, nature, and justifications. The term "right" it is a subject of philosophical controversy, with various perspectives on its precise meaning. Human rights encompass a wide array of rights, ranging from the right to a fair trial and protection against enslavement to free speech and the right to education.
However, there is disagreement among thinkers about which specific rights should be universally recognized as human rights.

Some argue that human rights should serve as a minimum standard to prevent the most egregious abuses, while others advocate for a higher standard that goes beyond mere protection and aims for the fulfillment of basic needs and dignity. Additionally, there are differing views on whether human rights are inherent and inherent to human beings or whether they are bestowed by a higher authority, such as a divine entity (Beitz, 2009).

In conclusion, the concept of human rights has wielded significant influence in international law and global discourse. It serves as a common moral language guiding public policy, but it also evokes ongoing debates about the specific rights included within its framework and their justifications. The notion of human rights remains a complex and evolving topic that continues to shape our understanding of justice, equality, and the dignity of all individuals.

Purpose and scope of the book

The purpose of the book "Unshackling Humanity: Human Rights in Africa and the Genesis of the UDHR" is to provide a comprehensive and insightful exploration of the history, importance, and impact of human rights in Africa,

with a particular focus on the emergence and significance of the Universal Declaration of Human Rights (UDHR). Through a nuanced examination of historical events, key figures, and pivotal moments, the book seeks to shed light on the struggles and achievements in promoting and protecting human rights in the African continent.

The scope of the book encompasses various aspects related to human rights in Africa, including:

i. Historical Context: The book delves into the historical context of human rights in Africa, examining pre-colonial societies with traditional systems of justice, the impact of European colonization on human rights, and the struggles for independence and national sovereignty.

ii.   The UDHR and Africa: A significant portion of the book is dedicated to exploring the Universal Declaration of Human Rights and its relevance to Africa. It provides an overview of the 30 articles of the UDHR and how it became a pivotal document in shaping human rights standards worldwide.

iii.   African Perspectives: The book highlights the contributions of African leaders, activists, and delegates in the drafting process of the UDHR. It emphasizes the distinct African human rights perspectives and the influence they had on the formulation of the declaration.

iv.   Adoption and Impact: The book examines the reception and adoption of the UDHR by African nations, as well as how it was incorporated into domestic legal systems. It showcases case studies of countries that directly cited the UDHR in their municipal constitutions, reflecting its tangible impact on the continent.

v.   Human Rights Challenges: The book addresses the human rights challenges faced by post-colonial Africa, including struggles for justice and accountability in the face of atrocities such as apartheid in South Africa and the genocide in Rwanda.

vi.   International Criminal Court (ICC) and Human Rights: It delves into the establishment and mandate of the ICC and its jurisdiction over human rights violations in Africa, alongside the criticisms and challenges the ICC has faced on the continent.

vii.   Advancements and Setbacks: The book presents success stories in promoting human rights in Africa, but also acknowledges persistent challenges and obstacles to progress. It explores the role of civil society, NGOs, and grassroots movements in advancing human rights.

viii.   Reflections and Future Prospects: The book assesses the impact of the UDHR on human rights in Africa and the influence of African perspectives on international law. It discusses ongoing efforts to strengthen human rights protection in the region and expresses hope for an empowered future through continued human rights advocacy.

The overall purpose of the book is to offer a comprehensive and well-researched account of human rights in Africa and its connection to the Universal Declaration of Human Rights. By providing a nuanced understanding of the challenges, advancements, and the ongoing struggle for human rights, the book aims to foster greater awareness, empathy, and commitment to upholding human rights principles in Africa and beyond.

Nyangatom Kids Playing In Muddy Water, Kangate, Omo Valley, Ethiopia
Courtesy: Eric Lafforgue, November 28, 2014

CHAPTER TWO

Historical Context of Human Rights in Africa

The historical context of human rights in Africa is a complex and multifaceted journey that spans millennia. Africa's diverse cultures and civilizations have developed their own systems of justice and social norms that often recognized the inherent value and dignity of individuals. However, the emergence of human rights as a modern concept in the region is shaped by historical events, including colonialism, struggles for independence, and the global human rights movement.

i. Pre-colonial Societies: Before the arrival of European colonizers, many African societies had established intricate systems of governance, customary laws, and traditions that provided a framework for justice and social order. These societies often recognized the rights of individuals within their communities, including the right to life, freedom from harm, and access to resources and communal well-being.

ii. Impact of European Colonization: The 19th and 20th centuries marked the era of European colonization in Africa. European powers imposed colonial rule, leading to profound disruptions in African societies and widespread human rights abuses. Exploitative practices, forced labor, land dispossession, and cultural suppression were common, undermining the rights and dignity of African populations.

iii. Struggles for Independence: As the wave of decolonization swept across Africa in the mid-20th century, various independence movements emerged. These movements were fueled by a desire for self-determination and the restoration of human rights and sovereignty. Leaders and activists fought against colonial oppression and sought to establish nations that upheld the principles of justice, equality, and human rights.

iv. Pan-Africanism: Pan-Africanism, a movement that sought unity and solidarity among Africans and people of African descent worldwide, played a crucial role in advocating for human rights and African dignity. Leaders like Kwame Nkrumah, Jomo Kenyatta, and Julius Nyerere were prominent figures in advancing the cause of human rights in Africa.

v. African Charter on Human and Peoples' Rights: In 1981, the African Charter on Human and Peoples' Rights was adopted by the Organization of African Unity (now the African Union). The charter affirmed the principles of human rights, including civil, political, economic, social, and cultural rights, and marked a significant step towards a regional human rights framework in Africa.

vi. Human Rights Challenges: Post-colonial Africa faced numerous human rights challenges, including political repression, civil conflicts, ethnic tensions, and economic disparities. Authoritarian regimes and military dictatorships in some countries led to widespread human rights abuses, stifling dissent and suppressing freedoms.

vii. Advancements and Progress: Despite the challenges, Africa has witnessed progress in promoting human rights. Many African nations have taken steps to incorporate human rights principles into their constitutions and legal systems. Regional human rights bodies, such as the African Commission on Human and Peoples' Rights, play a vital role in monitoring and advancing human rights in the region.

viii. Contemporary Human Rights Issues: Africa continues to grapple with contemporary human rights issues, including gender-based violence, discrimination, access to education and healthcare, economic inequality, and the protection of marginalized groups such as refugees and internally displaced persons.

ix. Wars in Africa: The continent has experienced various wars and conflicts, some of which have been devastating in their impact on human rights. From the Rwandan Genocide and the Congo Wars to the Sudanese Civil War and the Somali Civil War, these conflicts have resulted in mass atrocities, displacement, and gross violations of human rights. The use of child soldiers, sexual violence, and attacks on civilians have further exacerbated the human rights situation in conflict-affected regions.

x. Identity and Tribal Problems: Africa's diverse societies encompass a wide array of ethnicities, cultures, and identities. While this diversity enriches the continent, it has also led to challenges related to identity and tribal tensions. Ethnic conflicts, discrimination, and exclusion based on identity have at times undermined efforts to uphold human rights and foster inclusive societies. Building a cohesive and inclusive national identity that respects the rights of all individuals remains an ongoing task.

In the face of these challenges, the promotion and protection of human rights in Africa have been multifaceted and complex. The continent has made significant progress in recognizing human rights as fundamental principles enshrined in regional charters and national constitutions. African states have established institutions and mechanisms to address human rights concerns and improve accountability for human rights violations. However, the legacy of past conflicts and identity-related issues continue to impact the region's human rights landscape.

Promoting peace, reconciliation, and social cohesion remains essential to address the underlying causes of conflicts and identity-based tensions.

As Africa continues its journey towards upholding human rights for all its people, it is crucial to address the root causes of conflicts, promote intercultural dialogue, and ensure that institutions are strengthened to protect and advance human rights. The ongoing commitment of African nations, regional organizations, civil society, and the international community is vital to building a future where human rights are universally respected, and every individual's dignity is upheld.

In conclusion, the historical context of human rights in Africa reflects a complex interplay of indigenous principles, colonial legacies, struggles for independence, and modern efforts to advance human rights and social justice. While significant progress has been made, challenges persist, underscoring the ongoing importance of promoting and protecting human rights on the African continent.

Pre-colonial societies and traditional systems of justice

Pre-colonial societies in Africa were characterized by their incredible diversity and rich cultural heritage. The continent's vast expanse, ranging from the Sahara desert to lush rainforests, contributed to the development of distinct languages, customs, and traditions among different communities. From the great empires of Ghana, Mali, and Songhai in West Africa to the Kingdoms of Axum and Kush in East Africa, pre-colonial Africa was home to a plethora of advanced civilizations. These societies thrived through agricultural practices, trade, and craftsmanship, contributing to the continent's vibrant and dynamic history.

Great Mosque of Djenne in Pre colonial Mali
Source: *flickr, Uploaded on February 22, 2010*

In these pre-colonial societies, governance was typically organized around kinship and clan structures. Leaders, such as chiefs, kings, or queens, held positions of authority, and leadership roles were often passed down through hereditary lines. These leaders played pivotal roles in maintaining order, resolving disputes, and ensuring the well-being of their communities. Decisions were often made through consensus, with an emphasis on community involvement and consultation.

Trade and commerce were significant aspects of pre-colonial African societies. Long before the arrival of European colonizers, African communities engaged in extensive trade networks.

They exchanged a wide range of goods, including gold, ivory, salt, spices, textiles, and even slaves.

These trade routes connected Africa to various parts of the world, fostering cultural exchange and economic development. The flourishing trade contributed to the growth of urban centers and the development of specialized craftsmanship.

Religion and belief systems were central to the lives of pre-colonial Africans. The continent was home to diverse spiritual traditions, ranging from indigenous animistic beliefs to organized religions like Christianity and Islam, which were introduced through trade and contact with traders and travelers. These belief systems played a crucial role in shaping cultural practices, social norms, and governance structures, providing a sense of identity and cohesion within communities. Family and community bonds held significant importance in pre-colonial African societies. Extended families were the foundation of social structure, and communal values emphasized collective responsibility and mutual support. Individuals found belonging and security within their communities, and cooperation was vital for survival and progress.

Pre-colonial African societies had a profound impact on the continent's history and the development of its cultural, social, and political landscapes. While each society had its unique characteristics, they collectively contributed to the diversity and resilience of Africa's heritage. Understanding and appreciating the complexity of pre-colonial African societies are essential to recognizing the rich legacy that continues to shape the continent's identity and progress (Turchin and Jonathan, 2006). Below is a list of kingdoms in pre-colonial Africa, which existed before the Scramble for Africa (c. 1880–1914) when most of the continent came under the control of European powers

Some kingdoms, such as the Kingdom of Ardra in Benin, Buganda in Uganda, or the Kingdom of Bailundo in Angola, still exist today as non-sovereign monarchies, with varying legal and constitutional statuses within their respective countries.

i.   Kingdom of Benin (now part of modern-day Nigeria): The Kingdom of Benin was a powerful and highly developed kingdom in West Africa. It was known for its advanced bronze and ivory artwork, as well as its complex political and social structures.

ii.   Kingdom of Ghana (not to be confused with the modern nation of Ghana): The Kingdom of Ghana was one of the earliest and most powerful empires in West Africa. It was a center of trade and cultural exchange, controlling vast territories and resources.

iii.   Kingdom of Mali: The Kingdom of Mali was a prominent empire in West Africa, known for its wealth, advanced cities like Timbuktu, and famous rulers like Mansa Musa, who was renowned for his pilgrimage to Mecca and generous distribution of gold.

iv.   Kingdom of Songhai: Following the decline of Mali, the Kingdom of Songhai rose to prominence in West Africa. It was a major center of trade and Islamic learning and reached its peak during the reign of Emperor Askia Muhammad.

v.   Kingdom of Kongo (now part of modern-day Angola and the Democratic Republic of Congo): The Kingdom of Kongo was a powerful central African kingdom with a well-developed political and administrative structure, as well as a thriving trade network.

vi.   Kingdom of Zimbabwe (Great Zimbabwe): The Kingdom of Zimbabwe was known for its impressive stone structures, such as the Great Enclosure and the Hill Complex. It was an important trading center in southern Africa.

vii. Kingdom of Buganda (now part of modern-day Uganda): The Kingdom of Buganda was a powerful and centralized kingdom in East Africa, known for its organized bureaucracy and strong cultural identity.

viii. Kingdom of Ethiopia: Ethiopia has a long history as an ancient kingdom, and its monarchy traces its lineage back to biblical times. The Ethiopian Kingdom was known for its cultural and religious significance, including its connection to the Ethiopian Orthodox Church.

ix. Kingdom of Dahomey (now part of modern-day Benin): The Kingdom of Dahomey was a powerful and militaristic kingdom in West Africa. It was known for its strong and well-disciplined army, as well as its use of female warriors known as the Dahomey Amazons.

x. Kingdom of Zulu (now part of modern-day South Africa): The Kingdom of Zulu was a powerful and influential kingdom in southern Africa, known for its military prowess and expansion under leaders like Shaka Zulu.

These are just a few examples of the numerous kingdoms and empires that thrived in pre-colonial Africa. Each of these kingdoms contributed to the continent's rich history, cultural heritage, and political complexity. The legacy of these kingdoms continues to shape the identities and narratives of modern African nations.

Historian Jan Vansina's classification of Sub-Saharan African kingdoms provides valuable insights into the varying degrees of centralization of power in these historical polities. The categorization distinguishes five types of kingdoms based on the extent of control the king exerted over internal and external affairs:

i. Despotic Kingdoms: In despotic kingdoms, the king held direct control over both internal and external affairs. Examples of such kingdoms include Rwanda,

Ankole, Busoga, and the Kingdom of Kongo during the 16th century. The ruler's authority was centralized, and decisions were made without the intermediation of overseers or administrators.

ii. Regal Kingdoms: In regal kingdoms, the king maintained direct control over external affairs, while internal affairs were managed through a system of overseers or chiefs. The king and his chiefs often shared the same religion or belonged to the same social group, reinforcing cohesion within the ruling elite.

iii. Incorporative Kingdoms: Incorporative kingdoms were characterized by the king's control limited to external affairs, with no permanent administrative links to the chiefs of the provinces. After conquest, the existing hereditary chiefdoms in the provinces remained largely untouched. Examples of such kingdoms include the Bamileke, Lunda, Luba, and Lozi.

iv. Aristocratic Kingdoms: In aristocratic kingdoms, the primary link between central authority and the provinces was through the payment of tribute. These kingdoms displayed intermediate characteristics between regal kingdoms and federations. Examples of this type are the Kongo during the 17th century, as well as the Cazembe, Luapula, Kuba, Ngonde, Mlanje, Ha, Zinza, and Chagga states during the 18th century.

v. Federations: Federations were characterized by a council of elders, with the king serving as the first among equals (primus inter pares). The external affairs of the federation were regulated through this council. An example of such a federation is the Ashanti Union.

It is essential to note that the classification provided by Vansina specifically focuses on Sub-Saharan African kingdoms in Central, South, and East Africa.

The Islamic empires of North and Northeast Africa, such as the Caliphates and Sultanates, do not fall within this categorization and should be discussed as part of the Muslim world, given their distinctive political and religious characteristics.

Vansina's classification offers valuable insights into the diverse political structures and governance systems that existed in pre-colonial Africa. These kingdoms played pivotal roles in shaping the continent's history and cultural development and continue to be an important area of study for historians and scholars interested in African civilizations and societies (Vansina, 1962 pp. 324–335).

Traditional Systems of Justice

Traditional systems of justice, also known as customary or indigenous systems of justice, are legal and dispute resolution mechanisms that have been developed and practiced by various communities and societies over generations. These systems predate formal state-imposed legal structures and are deeply rooted in the cultural, social, and historical contexts of the communities they serve. Traditional systems of justice continue to play significant roles in many parts of the world, particularly in rural and remote areas, where state institutions may be limited in their reach.

Characteristics of Traditional Systems of Justice

Restorative and Community-Centered: Traditional systems of justice prioritize restoring harmony and balance within the community rather than focusing solely on punitive measures. Disputes and conflicts are seen as affecting the entire community, and the goal is to reconcile the parties involved and maintain social cohesion.

i. Informal and Oral: These systems are often informal and rely on oral traditions rather than written laws or formal legal codes. Disputes are resolved through dialogue, negotiation, and storytelling, with elders or community leaders playing crucial roles as mediators and arbitrators.

ii. Flexibility and Adaptability: Traditional systems of justice are often flexible and adaptable to the specific circumstances of each case. Decisions are based on the particular context, cultural norms, and the needs of the individuals involved.

iii. Inclusivity and Participation: Community members, regardless of their status, have the opportunity to participate in the decision-making process. The emphasis is on inclusivity and ensuring that all affected parties have a voice in resolving the dispute.

iv. Integration of Customary Practices: These systems often incorporate customary practices, rituals, and traditions that hold cultural and symbolic significance for the community. Such practices may reinforce the importance of adherence to local norms and values.

v. Relevance in Daily Life: Traditional systems of justice address a wide range of disputes and conflicts, including property disputes, family matters, marriage and divorce issues, and minor offenses. They are an integral part of daily life in many communities.

Challenges and Concerns

While traditional systems of justice have served as essential mechanisms for dispute resolution and maintaining social order, they also face some challenges and concerns:

i. Lack of Legal Protections: In some cases, traditional systems may not offer adequate protection for vulnerable individuals, particularly women, children, and marginalized groups. Customary norms and practices may perpetuate gender bias and discriminatory practices.

ii. Limited Access to Formal Justice: In areas where state legal systems are weak or inaccessible, traditional systems may be the primary means of resolving disputes. However, they may lack legal recognition and enforcement, leading to potential abuses or injustices.

iii.   Balancing with State Law: In countries with plural legal systems, reconciling traditional justice with state laws and human rights standards can be complex. Striking a balance between preserving cultural heritage and ensuring fundamental human rights is an ongoing challenge.

iv.   Preservation and Modernization: The continued viability of traditional systems may be threatened by modernization, urbanization, and external influences. Striking a balance between preserving valuable cultural heritage and adapting to changing social dynamics is essential.

In conclusion, traditional systems of justice have long been essential pillars of community life in many parts of the world. They reflect the cultural values, norms, and identity of the communities they serve. While they continue to play a significant role in dispute resolution and social cohesion, efforts to address challenges and ensure compatibility with human rights principles remain vital to achieve a just and inclusive legal landscape.

Impact of European colonization on human rights

European colonization had a profound impact on human rights in various parts of the world. Indigenous populations were subjected to forced labor and slavery, leading to immense suffering and the denial of basic human rights and dignity. The seizure of land from indigenous communities resulted in dispossession, displacement, and economic inequalities. Cultural suppression and assimilation led to the erosion of traditional knowledge and values, while violent conflicts and genocide caused the loss of countless lives and the destruction of entire communities.

Colonial powers established hierarchies based on race and ethnicity, leading to discrimination and marginalization of indigenous peoples and people of African descent.

Political rights were denied, as colonial authorities controlled political institutions and suppressed dissent. Economic exploitation of colonized regions further perpetuated poverty and deprivation among the local populations. The introduction of new diseases without immunity, such as smallpox and influenza, had devastating health impacts and contributed to population declines. Traditional legal and justice systems were replaced by colonial legal systems, resulting in a loss of autonomy in administering justice.

The legacies of European colonization continue to shape present-day human rights challenges, as historical injustices and inequalities persist. Addressing these issues, promoting social justice, and respecting the rights of indigenous and marginalized communities remain ongoing efforts in the post-colonial era. Acknowledging and learning from this dark chapter of history is crucial for building a more just and equitable world.

The African people have long experienced powerlessness, illiteracy, violence, hunger, and extreme poverty, which have been persistent challenges. Over the past five centuries, various strategies have been employed to exploit African human and natural resources. These strategies included the commodification of young Africans through the slave trade, the domination and control of trade by external powers, the destruction of African institutions, cultures, and religions, and the imposition of Christianity. African leadership and sovereignty were undermined, and the African people were deprived of their ownership over lands and economic resources, turning many into slaves. These exploitative practices were driven by a pursuit of private profit, leading to disastrous consequences for native Africans, as pointed out by Lonsdale in 1985.

Colonialism had a severely destructive impact on African colonies, as highlighted by Walter Rodney in his book "How Europe Underdeveloped Africa" (1982).

It weakened African economic infrastructure, educational systems, trade, markets, transportation, and currency. The reliance on monocultural economies created dependency and further dehumanized the African labor force and traders. Africans were forced to work for colonizers on their own lands for meager wages, as documented by Ocheni and Nwankwo in 2012.

The legacy of colonialism, along with state terrorism and racism, has contributed to the persistent underdevelopment and extreme poverty faced by the African people, despite achieving "flag" independence in the mid-20th century. Native Africans' land, labor, and other resources were exploited by colonizers for their own accumulation of wealth and power, often without any sense of remorse, as Chomsky emphasized in 1993. It is crucial for the present generation of Africans and people worldwide to acknowledge and recognize the crimes committed by colonial states in pursuit of profit and territorial acquisition, which resulted in human rights violations and various socio-economic, cultural, and political problems for indigenous people, as highlighted by Asafa in 2015.

Struggles for independence and national sovereignty in Africa

Nationalism and the struggle for political independence in Africa have been a continuous and complex process, spanning across pre-colonial, colonial, and postcolonial periods. The nature and character of these struggles varied based on the aspirations of the people and the unique circumstances of each era. Before the European imperialist incursion in the late 19th century, pre-colonial African kingdoms and states actively resisted the invaders to protect their local independence and sovereignty. They fought to preserve their cultures, traditions, and political autonomy against colonial encroachment.

During the colonial period, nationalist movements emerged, seeking self-rule and liberation from colonial domination. In some regions, like British West Africa, independence was achieved through constitutional and relatively peaceful means, with negotiations and agreements leading to the transfer of power from colonial authorities to local leaders. However, in other parts of Africa, such as Lusophone Africa (Portuguese-speaking territories) and the Maghreb, the road to independence was marked by significant violence and bloodshed. Armed liberation struggles and protracted conflicts characterized the fight against colonial rule in these regions.

The attainment of independence was a momentous achievement for many African countries, but it also brought challenges in nation-building and national development. The legacy of colonialism, including social divisions, economic disparities, and political instabilities, had a lasting negative impact on the postcolonial African states. Nation-building and national development have been hindered by the legacies of colonial exploitation, as well as internal struggles for power and resources. The postcolonial African states had to contend with the complexities of forging cohesive national identities and overcoming the divisions imposed by colonial boundaries. Additionally, external influences, such as neocolonialism and geopolitical interests, continued to shape the trajectory of African nations even after independence. The quest for true self-determination and economic independence has been an ongoing struggle for many African countries.

In conclusion, nationalism and the quest for political independence in Africa have been part of a long and multifaceted journey.

While some regions achieved independence through peaceful means, others faced violent struggles.

Regardless of the path to independence, the challenges of colonial legacies and nation-building have impacted the development of postcolonial African states. The continent continues to strive for genuine nation-building and sustainable development, seeking to overcome the lasting effects of colonialism and chart a prosperous future (Michael, 1968).

The struggles for independence and national sovereignty in Africa were pivotal moments in the continent's history, marked by widespread movements and efforts to break free from colonial rule and assert self-determination. These struggles were driven by a desire for political autonomy, economic independence, and the restoration of African identity and cultural heritage. Here are some key aspects of the struggles for independence and national sovereignty in Africa:

i.   Pan-Africanism and Nationalism: Pan-Africanism, a movement advocating for unity and solidarity among Africans and people of African descent worldwide, played a significant role in fostering a sense of collective identity and promoting the idea of self-governance. Nationalist leaders emerged in various African countries, rallying their people around the common goal of independence.

ii. Anti-Colonial Movements: Anti-colonial movements took various forms, including protests, strikes, boycotts, and armed resistance. African leaders and activists, such as Kwame Nkrumah in Ghana, Jomo Kenyatta in Kenya, Julius Nyerere in Tanzania, and Nelson Mandela in South Africa, became iconic figures in the fight against colonial oppression.

iii. Formation of Political Parties: Political parties advocating for independence and national sovereignty were formed across the continent. These parties mobilized support through grassroots organizing and political campaigns, demanding an end to colonial rule and the establishment of self-governing nations.

iv. Decolonization: The post-World War II era saw a significant wave of decolonization in Africa. As European colonial powers faced economic and political challenges after the war, the momentum for independence in African colonies intensified. Ghana's independence in 1957, led by Nkrumah, was a pivotal moment that inspired other African nations to follow suit.

v. Peaceful Transitions and Armed Struggles: While some African countries achieved independence through peaceful negotiations, others engaged in armed struggles against colonial forces. Algeria's war for independence against France and Mozambique's struggle against Portuguese colonial rule are notable examples of armed liberation movements.

vi. Continental Solidarity: African countries and leaders supported each other's struggles for independence, often providing moral and material support. The establishment of the Organization of African Unity (OAU) in 1963 aimed to promote unity and cooperation among African nations and further the cause of decolonization.

vii. Post-Independence Challenges: While achieving independence was a monumental achievement, newly independent African nations faced various challenges, including nation-building, economic development, and managing ethnic and regional diversity.

viii. Legacy and Pan-African Cooperation: The struggles for independence left a lasting legacy, shaping the political, social, and cultural landscape of modern Africa. Pan-African cooperation and regional integration continue to be important objectives for the continent's progress.

The struggles for independence and national sovereignty in Africa were significant milestones in the continent's history, leading to the birth of numerous sovereign nations and fostering a sense of pride, identity, and unity among African peoples. However, the journey toward achieving sustainable development and prosperity remains ongoing, as the continent grapples with various socio-economic and political challenges.

Early human rights movements in Africa emerged as a response to colonialism, oppression, and the denial of basic rights and freedoms to the African population. These movements were led by African leaders, intellectuals, and activists who advocated for social justice, equality, and the recognition of human rights for all Africans. Some key early human rights movements in Africa include:

CHAPTER THREE

Early Human Rights Movements in Africa

Anticolonial struggles for self-determination had significant impact on the development of the idea of universal human rights. In the second half of the twentieth century, colonized people drew on the emergent language of universal human rights in their ideological struggles against European imperialism and to articulate demands for independence. Anticolonial movements in Africa were among the first mass movements to draw on the language of human rights in the post-Second World War era. Yet, some scholars have argued that anti-colonialism was not a human rights movement because its primary aim was collective national liberation rather than the reduction of state power over the individual (Patterson, 1995).

Pan-African Congresses: The Pan-African Congresses, initiated by African and diaspora intellectuals and activists, were significant gatherings that advocated for the rights of Africans and people of African descent worldwide. The first Pan-African Congress was held in 1900 in London, followed by subsequent congresses in different locations. These congresses laid the foundation for the Pan-African movement, which aimed to promote unity, solidarity, and collective action among Africans to address common challenges.

1. Ethiopian Resistance: Ethiopia's resistance against Italian colonialism, particularly during the First Italo-Ethiopian War (1895-1896), was a powerful symbol of African resistance against European imperialism. Emperor Menelik II's victory at the Battle of Adwa in 1896 demonstrated that Africans were capable of defending their sovereignty and challenging colonial powers.

2. Anti-Apartheid Movement: The anti-apartheid movement in South Africa emerged as a powerful

struggle against racial segregation and discrimination imposed by the white minority government. Activists like Nelson Mandela, Albertina Sisulu, and Walter Sisulu, among others, played crucial roles in advocating for civil rights and human dignity for all South Africans.

3. Negritude Movement: The Negritude movement, led by African and Caribbean intellectuals and writers, emphasized the pride and celebration of African cultural heritage and identity. It aimed to challenge colonial narratives that denigrated African history and culture, promoting a positive self-image for Africans.

4. Kenyan Land and Freedom Army (Mau Mau): The Mau Mau uprising in Kenya during the 1950s was a resistance movement against British colonial rule and land dispossession. The Mau Mau sought to reclaim their ancestral lands and challenge oppressive colonial policies.

5. West African Nationalist Movements: In British West Africa, nationalist movements emerged in countries like Ghana, Nigeria, and Sierra Leone. Leaders like Kwame Nkrumah, Nnamdi Azikiwe, and Obafemi Awolowo advocated for independence and self-governance, paving the way for the decolonization of the region.

6. North African Independence Movements: In North Africa, countries like Tunisia, Algeria, and Morocco also witnessed nationalist movements against French colonial rule. These movements sought to achieve independence and self-determination for their respective countries.

These early human rights movements in Africa laid the groundwork for the struggle for independence and national sovereignty, as well as the promotion of human rights and social justice on the continent.

They played a crucial role in shaping Africa's history and identity, and their legacies continue to inspire contemporary human rights activism in Africa.

Decolonization in Africa

Decolonization in Africa refers to the process through which African countries gained independence from European colonial powers. It was a significant historical movement that reshaped the political landscape of the continent and marked the end of formal colonial rule. Decolonization in Africa occurred primarily in the mid-20th century, following the aftermath of World War II, when the tide of global politics and international sentiment shifted in favor of self-determination and anti-colonial struggles. Here are key aspects of the decolonization process in Africa

Meaning of Decolonization

Decolonization is the process of undoing colonialism, wherein imperial nations establish and dominate foreign territories, often overseas. However, the exact meaning and scope of the term are subjects of debate among scholars. Some focus on decolonization as independence movements in colonies and the collapse of global colonial empires. This perspective emphasizes political emancipation and the establishment of sovereign states.

Others adopt a broader approach to decolonization, considering economic, cultural, and psychological aspects of the colonial experience. This extended meaning includes efforts to challenge and dismantle colonial structures of power and knowledge, even after achieving political independence. Scholars who follow this line of thought, known as the decoloniality school, advocate for the decolonization of knowledge and the recognition of indigenous and post-colonial worldviews (BETTS, 2012).

However, this expanded view of decolonization has faced criticism from some quarters.

Critics argue that such broad interpretations may overlook the agency and conscious choices made by people in former colonies, who may selectively adopt and adapt elements from colonial rule for their own purposes. Additionally, some scholars caution against essentializing identities or perpetuating reified notions of cultural heritage in the pursuit of decolonization. They advocate for nuanced and context-specific approaches that recognize the complexity and diversity of post-colonial experiences (Naicker, 2023).

Overall, the term decolonization encompasses a wide range of perspectives and approaches, from political independence to challenging colonial power structures and cultural knowledge paradigms. Debates surrounding decolonization continue to shape academic discourse and practical efforts to address the legacies of colonialism in contemporary societies (Nabobo-Baba, 2006).

The United Nations (UN) recognizes the fundamental right to self-determination as a core requirement for decolonization, whether it is exercised with or without achieving political independence. A UN General Assembly Resolution in 1960 specifically characterized colonial foreign rule as a violation of human rights. Even in states that have won independence, Indigenous people living under settler colonialism continue to demand decolonization and self-determination (Roy, 2001).

Decolonization has a long historical trajectory, with examples dating back to ancient times, as seen in the writings of Thucydides. However, there have been particularly active periods of decolonization in modern history. These include the breakup of various empires following World War I and World War II, leading to the independence of numerous African and Asian nations, as well as the dissolution of the Soviet Union at the end of the Cold War (R Strayer, 2001).

Early studies of decolonization emerged in the 1960s and 1970s, with influential works like Frantz Fanon's "The Wretched of the Earth" (1961) addressing key aspects of the decolonization process. Subsequent studies further explored economic disparities resulting from colonialism and the devastating impact on indigenous cultures. Ngũgĩ wa Thiong'o's book "Decolonising the Mind" (1986) delved into the cultural and linguistic legacies of colonialism (BETTS, 2012).

Beyond political and economic aspects, "decolonization" has also been used to refer to the process of freeing the colonized from the ideas and perceptions imposed by colonizers that made them feel inferior. This intellectual decolonization is an ongoing struggle to reclaim and affirm cultural identities and narratives that have been marginalized or suppressed during colonial rule.

Issues related to decolonization continue to be relevant and are actively discussed in contemporary contexts, particularly in the Americas and South Africa, where they are increasingly examined under the term "decoloniality." These discussions highlight the continued relevance and complexities of decolonization as societies seek to address historical injustices and create more inclusive and equitable futures (Hodgkinson, 2019).

Decolonization in Africa

The decolonization of North Africa and sub-Saharan Africa indeed occurred in the mid-to-late 1950s, marking a significant and tumultuous period in the history of the continent. This process involved the granting of independence to numerous African nations that were formerly under European colonial rule. The decolonization process in Africa was characterized by widespread unrest, organized revolts, and struggles for self-determination.

In North Africa, countries like Algeria, Tunisia, and Morocco experienced intense and protracted battles for independence from French colonial rule. The Algerian War of Independence (1954-1962) was particularly notable for its scale and violence, with the Algerian people fighting for their sovereignty and national identity.

In sub-Saharan Africa, countries such as Angola, the Democratic Republic of Congo (then known as the Belgian Congo), and Kenya witnessed similar movements for independence. The Congolese independence struggle culminated in the country gaining independence from Belgium in 1960, while Angola achieved its independence from Portugal in 1975 after a prolonged armed struggle.

In British Kenya, the Mau Mau rebellion (1952-1960) was a significant uprising against British colonial rule, demanding land rights and political representation. The resistance in Kenya was met with brutal repression from British authorities, leading to a deep divide and lasting scars on the nation's history (Willian, 1982).

The decolonization of Africa was a rapid and largely unforeseen process, catching both colonial powers and African societies by surprise. The lack of preparation for independence led to challenges in nation-building and governance after independence was attained. The suddenness of decolonization also created tensions and complexities in defining national borders, as colonial boundaries often did not align with pre-existing ethnic or tribal territories.

Despite the challenges, the decolonization of Africa brought about a new era of self-determination, national pride, and independence. However, the legacy of colonialism, including economic disparities, political instabilities, and social divisions, continued to shape postcolonial African nations and influence their trajectories in the decades that followed (John, 2014).

In 1945, Africa had only four independent countries: Egypt, Ethiopia, Liberia, and South Africa. After World War II, former Italian colonies in Africa were occupied by France and the UK. Libya became an independent kingdom in 1951, while Eritrea was merged with Ethiopia in 1952. Italian Somaliland was governed by the UK and later by Italy until gaining independence in 1960.

By 1977, European colonial rule in mainland Africa had ended, and most of Africa's island countries had also become independent, except for Réunion and Mayotte, which remained part of France. However, Rhodesia and South Africa continued to disenfranchise their black majorities until 1979 and 1994, respectively. Namibia, the last UN Trust Territory in Africa, gained independence from South Africa in 1990. The majority of independent African countries retained the colonial borders established during the colonial era. Some exceptions include Morocco, which merged French Morocco with Spanish Morocco, and Somalia, formed by the merger of British Somaliland and Italian Somaliland. Eritrea initially merged with Ethiopia in 1952 but became an independent country in 1993.

Most independent African countries adopted republican forms of government. However, a few countries, like Morocco, Lesotho, and Eswatini, retained their monarchies under dynasties that predate colonial rule. Some countries, such as Burundi, Egypt, Libya, and Tunisia, gained independence as monarchies but later transitioned to republics after the monarchs were deposed.

The process of decolonization and the establishment of independent African nations was a complex and transformative period in the continent's history.

It marked the end of European colonial domination and the beginning of self-determination and nation-building for African countries. However, the legacy of colonialism continued to influence the political, social, and economic dynamics of many African nations even after gaining independence (Willian, 1982).

African countries engage in various forms of cooperation through multi-state associations aimed at fostering regional integration, economic development, and collaboration on shared challenges. The African Union (AU) serves as the continent's primary regional organization, comprising all 55 African states. Additionally, several regional associations of states exist, each with specific goals and memberships. Some of these organizations have overlapping memberships, reflecting the interconnectedness of African nations.

Examples of regional associations in Africa

East African Community (EAC): Comprising Burundi, Kenya, Rwanda, South Sudan, Tanzania, and Uganda, the EAC aims to promote economic integration and cooperation among its member states.

Southern African Development Community (SADC): SADC brings together 16 southern African countries, focusing on economic development, poverty alleviation, and regional integration.

Economic Community of West African States (ECOWAS): ECOWAS includes 15 West African nations, working towards economic and political integration, peace, and security in the region.

These regional organizations are essential in promoting cooperation, trade, and stability within their respective regions. They facilitate the development of shared policies, protocols, and initiatives that address regional challenges, such as conflicts, economic disparities, and infrastructure development.

Historically, many African countries gained their independence from colonial powers in the mid-20th century. The process of decolonization led to the formation of newly independent states across the continent. Some examples of African countries gaining independence from their respective colonial powers include:

United Kingdom: Sudan (1956); Ghana (1957); Nigeria (1960); Sierra Leone and Tanganyika (1961); Uganda (1962); Kenya and the Sultanate of Zanzibar (1963); Malawi and Zambia (1964); Gambia and Rhodesia (now Zimbabwe) (1965); Botswana and Lesotho (1966); Mauritius and Swaziland (1968); Seychelles (1976).

France: Morocco and Tunisia (1956); Guinea (1958); Cameroon, Togo, Mali, Senegal, Madagascar, Benin, Niger, Burkina Faso, Ivory Coast, Chad, the Central African Republic, the Republic of the Congo, Gabon, and Mauritania (1960); Algeria (1962); Comoros (1975); Djibouti (1977).

Spain: Equatorial Guinea (1968).

Portugal: Guinea-Bissau (1974); Mozambique, Cape Verde, São Tomé and Príncipe, and Angola (1975).

Belgium: Democratic Republic of the Congo (1960); Burundi, and Rwanda (1962).

The process of decolonization was a significant turning point in African history, as it marked the end of colonial rule and paved the way for the establishment of independent African states.

Early Human Rights Movements in Africa

Early human rights movements in Africa emerged during the colonial and pre-independence periods when African people and activists started advocating for their rights, equality, and dignity. These movements laid the foundation for the promotion of human rights across the continent and played a crucial role in shaping Africa's struggle for independence and post-colonial governance.

1. Pan-Africanism: One of the earliest forms of African human rights movements was the Pan-African

movement, which began in the late 19th and early 20th centuries. Pan-Africanism aimed to unite people of African descent worldwide, promote solidarity, and fight against racial discrimination and colonial oppression. Leaders like Marcus Garvey, W.E.B. Du Bois, and George Padmore advocated for the rights of Africans and sought to challenge colonial domination through political and intellectual activism.

2. African Nationalism: As African countries faced colonial rule, nationalist movements emerged, demanding self-determination and independence. These movements sought to empower African people and challenge the oppressive colonial systems. Leaders such as Jomo Kenyatta in Kenya, Kwame Nkrumah in Ghana, and Julius Nyerere in Tanzania played significant roles in advancing the cause of African nationalism and human rights.

3. Anti-Apartheid Movement: In South Africa, the anti-apartheid movement became a powerful force against racial segregation and discrimination. Activists like Nelson Mandela, Walter Sisulu, and Albertina Sisulu, among others, led campaigns for civil rights and equal treatment for all South Africans, regardless of race.

4. Human Rights Declarations: During the early 20th century, African leaders and intellectuals participated in various international conferences and forums, advocating for human rights and self-determination for African people. The Universal Declaration of Human Rights (UDHR), adopted in 1948 by the United Nations, laid the groundwork for the protection of human rights globally, including in Africa.

5. Trade Unions and Labor Movements: Trade unions and labor movements also played a role in advancing workers' rights and social justice in Africa during the colonial era. These movements sought better working

conditions, fair wages, and an end to exploitative labor practices.

6. Women's Rights Movements: Women in Africa were also active in early human rights movements, advocating for gender equality, education, and the right to participate in political and social spheres. Pioneering African women, like Funmilayo Ransome-Kuti in Nigeria and Charlotte Maxeke in South Africa, were at the forefront of these movements.

These early human rights movements in Africa laid the groundwork for the continent's continued struggle for human rights and social justice. They inspired later generations of activists and leaders to continue advocating for the rights and dignity of all Africans, contributing to the ongoing evolution of human rights protection and promotion in the region.

African leaders and activists that advocated for human rights in Africa

Numerous African leaders and activists played pivotal roles in the fight for independence from colonial rule, leading their countries towards self-determination and sovereignty. These individuals were instrumental in shaping the course of African history and inspiring movements for freedom and liberation. Some of the key African leaders and activists who fought for independence include:

1. Kwame Nkrumah (Ghana): Nkrumah was a visionary leader and a driving force behind Ghana's independence movement. As the leader of the Convention People's Party, he led Ghana to become the first sub-Saharan African country to gain independence from colonial rule in 1957.

2. Jomo Kenyatta (Kenya): Kenyatta was a prominent anti-colonial activist and the leader of the Kenya African Union (KAU). He played a crucial role in Kenya's struggle for independence, which was achieved in 1963.

3. Julius Nyerere (Tanzania): Nyerere was a charismatic leader and the founding father of Tanzania. As the leader of the Tanganyika African National Union (TANU), he led the country to independence from British colonial rule in 1961.

4. Ahmed Sékou Touré (Guinea): Touré was a charismatic leader and the first president of Guinea. Under his leadership, Guinea gained independence from France in 1958, making it the first French-speaking African country to achieve independence.

5. Patrice Lumumba (Democratic Republic of the Congo): Lumumba was a passionate advocate for Congolese independence and the first democratically elected prime minister of the Democratic Republic of the Congo. Despite his brief tenure, he remains a symbol of the country's struggle for self-rule.

6. Amílcar Cabral (Guinea-Bissau and Cape Verde): Cabral was a prominent anti-colonial leader and the founder of the African Party for the Independence of Guinea and Cape Verde (PAIGC). He led the successful liberation struggle against Portuguese colonial rule, resulting in the independence of Guinea-Bissau in 1973 and Cape Verde in 1975.

7. Nelson Mandela (South Africa): Mandela's leadership and unwavering commitment to justice and equality made him a global icon in the fight against apartheid in South Africa. His efforts, along with those of other anti-apartheid activists, led to the end of apartheid and the establishment of a democratic South Africa in 1994.

8. Samora Machel (Mozambique): Machel was a revolutionary leader and the first president of independent Mozambique. He led the Mozambique Liberation Front (FRELIMO) in their struggle against Portuguese colonial rule, culminating in the country's independence in 1975.

These leaders, along with countless other activists and revolutionaries, were instrumental in the fight for independence across Africa. Their resilience, sacrifices, and determination continue to inspire movements for freedom, equality, and progress on the continent and beyond.

Pre-UDHR human rights declarations and conventions
Before the adoption of the Universal Declaration of Human Rights (UDHR) in 1948, there were several pre-UDHR human rights declarations and conventions that laid the groundwork for the recognition and protection of human rights. These early documents contributed to the evolution of human rights principles and influenced the drafting of the UDHR. Some notable pre-UDHR human rights declarations and conventions include:

1. Magna Carta (1215): Although not a human rights declaration in the modern sense, Magna Carta was a significant historical document that laid the foundation for the rule of law and limited the powers of the monarchy in medieval England. It established the principle that even the king was subject to the law, and it paved the way for the protection of individual rights and liberties.

2. English Bill of Rights (1689): This document, enacted after the Glorious Revolution in England, affirmed certain civil liberties and limited the powers of the monarchy. It emphasized the right to petition the government, the right to bear arms, and the prohibition of cruel and unusual punishment.

3. Declaration of the Rights of Man and of the Citizen (1789): Adopted during the French Revolution, this declaration emphasized the principles of liberty, equality, and fraternity. It proclaimed that all individuals are born free and equal in rights and established the rights to liberty, property, security, and resistance to oppression.

4. United States Bill of Rights (1791): The first ten amendments to the United States Constitution, known as the Bill of Rights, enshrined fundamental rights and freedoms, including freedom of speech, religion, and the right to a fair trial.

5. Seneca Falls Declaration of Sentiments (1848): This declaration emerged from the first women's rights convention in the United States and advocated for women's equality and suffrage. It drew inspiration from earlier human rights documents and helped pave the way for the recognition of women's rights as human rights.

6. International Labour Organization (ILO) Conventions: The ILO, established in 1919, adopted numerous conventions promoting labor rights and social justice. These conventions addressed issues such as child labor, forced labor, working hours, and collective bargaining rights.

While these pre-UDHR declarations and conventions addressed specific aspects of human rights, the Universal Declaration of Human Rights represented a comprehensive and universal framework that brought together a broad range of rights and principles applicable to all individuals, regardless of their nationality, ethnicity, or other status. The UDHR marked a historic milestone in the global recognition and protection of human rights and continues to serve as a guiding document in the promotion of human dignity and equality worldwide.

Magna Carta

Magna Carta Libertatum, commonly known as Magna Carta, is a historic royal charter of rights agreed to by King John of England on June 15, 1215, at Runnymede, near Windsor. The charter was first drafted by Cardinal Stephen Langton, the Archbishop of Canterbury, as a means to reconcile King John with a group of rebel barons who were dissatisfied with his rule.

Magna Carta aimed to address various grievances and promises made by the king, including the protection of church rights, safeguarding the barons from illegal imprisonment, ensuring access to swift justice, and placing limitations on feudal payments to the Crown. These commitments were intended to be upheld through the establishment of a council of 25 barons.

However, both King John and the rebel barons failed to honor their commitments, leading to a breakdown in the agreement. Pope Innocent III subsequently annulled the charter, which further exacerbated tensions and culminated in the outbreak of the First Barons' War.

While Magna Carta did not achieve its immediate goals, it marked a significant milestone in the evolution of constitutional rights and the rule of law. Over time, its principles became central to the development of English common law and the protection of individual liberties. It laid the foundation for the idea that even the king was subject to the law and that certain rights should be respected and protected for all individuals.

Magna Carta's influence transcended its original context, inspiring later generations to champion the principles of liberty, justice, and human rights. It is often regarded as a symbol of resistance against oppressive rule and a pivotal document in the broader history of human rights and democratic governance (Peter, 2015).

After King John's death, the regency government led by his young son, Henry III, reissued Magna Carta in 1216. However, this version had some of its more radical provisions removed in an attempt to garner political support. Despite their efforts, the reissued charter did not achieve its intended goal. When the First Barons' War ended in 1217, Magna Carta was included in the peace treaty agreed at Lambeth. It was at this point that the document acquired the name "Magna Carta" (meaning "Great Charter") to distinguish it from the smaller Charter of the Forest, which was issued simultaneously.

In 1225, King Henry III found himself in need of funds and reissued Magna Carta once again.

This time, he offered the charter in exchange for a grant of new taxes. The document was reissued multiple times by successive monarchs as a way to assert their commitment to its principles. King Edward I, Henry III's son, repeated this practice in 1297 and formally confirmed Magna Carta as part of England's statute law. This confirmed its status as a key component of English political life.

Over time, as England's fledgling Parliament passed new laws and the country's political landscape evolved, Magna Carta gradually lost some of its practical significance. Nonetheless, it remained an important symbol of the principles of justice, fairness, and the rule of law. The charter's enduring legacy was reflected in its periodic renewal by each new monarch, demonstrating its continuing importance in the country's governance.

While its specific provisions have been superseded by subsequent laws and legal developments, Magna Carta's enduring impact on the development of constitutional rights, individual liberties, and the idea that even the king is subject to the law continues to resonate in the fields of human rights and democratic governance. It remains a treasured historical document and a symbol of the enduring struggle for freedom and justice.

In the late 16th century, there was a notable resurgence of interest in Magna Carta among lawyers and historians. During this time, there was a belief that an ancient English constitution, dating back to the Anglo-Saxon era, had safeguarded individual freedoms. These scholars argued that the Norman invasion of 1066 had disrupted these rights, and Magna Carta was seen as an effort to restore them. As a result, the charter was considered a vital foundation for the powers of Parliament and important legal principles like habeas corpus.

While this historical interpretation was flawed, it was influential during the early 17th century, with jurists like Sir Edward Coke using Magna Carta extensively to challenge the divine right of kings. This use of the charter was met with resistance from both King James I and his son, Charles I, who sought to suppress discussions related to Magna Carta.

Despite attempts to suppress it, the political myth surrounding Magna Carta and its protection of ancient personal liberties persisted after the Glorious Revolution of 1688 and well into the 19th century. The charter's influence extended beyond England and had a profound impact on the early American colonists in the Thirteen Colonies. When the United States Constitution was being formulated, Magna Carta served as an inspiration and model for the protection of individual rights and liberties in the new republic.

Victorian historians later conducted research that revealed the original 1215 charter primarily focused on the relationship between the monarch and the barons rather than the rights of ordinary people. Nevertheless, Magna Carta remained a powerful and iconic document, even after most of its content was repealed from the statute books in the 19th and 20th centuries.

Though the original 1215 Magna Carta is no longer in force as it was repealed, four of its clauses (1 [part], 13, 39, and 40) were enshrined in the reissued 1297 Magna Carta and continue to remain in force in England and Wales (designated as clauses 1, 9, and 29 of the 1297 statute). This recognition of certain clauses reflects the enduring significance of Magna Carta in the legal and constitutional history of England and its lasting impact on the protection of rights and liberties.

Magna Carta continues to hold significant symbolic importance in the modern world, frequently cited by politicians and activists as a testament to liberty and individual rights. It commands immense respect from the British and American legal communities, with Lord Denning describing it as "the greatest constitutional document of all times — the foundation of the freedom of the individual against the arbitrary authority of the despot."

In the 21st century, four exemplifications of the original 1215 Magna Carta still exist, with two housed at the British Library, one at Lincoln Castle, and another at Salisbury Cathedral.

Additionally, a few subsequent charters are held in public and private ownership, including copies of the 1297 charter in both the United States and Australia. While scholars today refer to the charter's 63 numbered "clauses," this numbering system was introduced by Sir William Blackstone in 1759 and is a modern convention.

The original Magna Carta comprised a single, long, and unbroken text. To commemorate the 800th anniversary of Magna Carta, the four original 1215 charters were displayed together at the British Library on 3 February 2015, underscoring the enduring significance of this historic document in shaping the principles of freedom and justice that continue to resonate in contemporary society Danziger and Gillingham, 2004).

English Bill of Rights (1689)
The Bill of Rights 1689, also known as the Bill of Rights 1688, is a crucial Act of the Parliament of England that enshrined certain fundamental civil rights and clarified the line of succession to the Crown. It holds significant importance in English constitutional law (Schwoerer, 1990).
Inspired by the ideas of political theorist John Locke, the Bill establishes a constitutional requirement for the Crown to seek the consent of the people represented in Parliament. It places limits on the powers of the monarch and affirms the rights of Parliament, including regular sessions, free elections, and parliamentary privilege.
Additionally, it outlines individual rights, such as the prohibition of cruel and unusual punishment and the right to refuse payment of taxes imposed without Parliament's approval. Furthermore, the Bill condemns specific misdeeds of King James II of England.On 16 December 1689, the Bill of Rights received royal assent. It essentially formalizes the Declaration of Right presented by the Convention Parliament to William III and Mary II in February 1689, inviting them to become joint sovereigns of England.
In the United Kingdom, the Bill is regarded as a fundamental document of the uncodified British constitution, along with other significant historical texts like Magna Carta, the Petition of Right, the Habeas Corpus Act 1679, and the Parliament Acts of 1911 and 1949.

In Scotland, a similar document called the Claim of Right Act 1689 applies. The Bill of Rights has been influential globally and served as a model for the United States Bill of Rights, the United Nations Declaration of Human Rights, and the European Convention on Human Rights. It remains in effect in all Commonwealth realms, as amended by the Perth Agreement, along with the Act of Settlement 1701 (Adams etal; 2017).

Declaration of the Rights of Man and of the Citizen (1789)
The Declaration of the Rights of Man and of the Citizen, adopted in 1789, is a fundamental document of the French Revolution that lays out the principles of liberty, equality, and fraternity. It was drafted by the National Assembly of France and represents a key milestone in the development of modern human rights.

The Declaration proclaims that all individuals are born free and equal in rights. It recognizes that these rights are universal and inalienable, applying to every human being without discrimination. The document enshrines the natural rights of individuals, which include liberty, property, security, and resistance to oppression. It also emphasizes the principles of popular sovereignty and the rule of law, stating that government exists to protect and uphold the rights of the people.

Furthermore, the Declaration advocates for the separation of powers and the accountability of public officials to the citizens.

It stresses the importance of public participation in decision-making processes and condemns arbitrary and despotic rule.

The Declaration proclaims the right to freedom of expression, freedom of religion, and the right to a fair trial.

The Declaration of the Rights of Man and of the Citizen served as an influential model for subsequent declarations and constitutions around the world. It played a significant role in shaping the modern concept of human rights and became a cornerstone of the principles of democratic governance and individual freedoms.

The Declaration of the Rights of Man and of the Citizen, drafted in 1789 during the French Revolution, is a significant human rights document that emerged from the ideals of the Enlightenment. It served as a fundamental statement of the principles that guided the revolution and had a profound impact on the conception of individual freedoms and democracy, not only in Europe but also worldwide

The document was influenced by Enlightenment philosophers and thinkers who promoted the idea of natural rights, asserting that these rights are universal and inherent to all human beings, regardless of time or place. It sought to establish a society where individuals enjoyed fundamental civil rights protected equally under the law. The Declaration advocated for the principles of liberty, equality, and fraternity, reflecting the aspirations of the French Revolution for a more just and democratic society (Kopstein, 2000). .

Marquis de Lafayette initially contributed to the drafting, but the majority of the final text was the work of Abbé Sieyès. The Declaration laid the groundwork for the concept of human rights as inalienable and fundamental to human existence, emphasizing the importance of individual liberties and equal protection under the law.

Incorporated at the beginning of the Fourth French Republic's constitution in 1946 and the Fifth Republic's constitution in 1958, the Declaration holds the status of constitutional law, serving as a cornerstone of French governance and reaffirming the importance of human rights for every citizen.

Its influence and legacy extend far beyond the borders of France, shaping the discourse on human rights and democratic ideals worldwide (Fremont-Barnes, 2007).

United States Bill of Rights (1791)

The United States Bill of Rights, adopted in 1791, is a crucial set of amendments to the United States Constitution. It was designed to protect the individual liberties and rights of American citizens from potential abuses by the federal government. The Bill of Rights consists of the first ten amendments to the Constitution and was drafted in response to concerns about the lack of specific protections for individual freedoms in the original Constitution.

The Bill of Rights guarantees various essential rights, including freedom of speech, religion, and the press, the right to bear arms, and the right to a fair and speedy trial by jury. It also safeguards against unreasonable searches and seizures, protects individuals from self-incrimination, and ensures the right to due process of law. Additionally, the Bill of Rights reserves certain rights to the states and the people, ensuring a balance of power between the federal government and the states.

The adoption of the Bill of Rights was a significant moment in American history, as it solidified the principles of individual liberty and limited government at the core of the nation's founding. These amendments have played a crucial role in shaping the legal landscape and protecting the rights and freedoms of American citizens for over two centuries. The United States Bill of Rights continues to be a foundational document in American governance, and its principles have influenced human rights and constitutional developments around the world.

The United States Bill of Rights, consisting of the first ten amendments to the U.S. Constitution, was proposed and adopted to address concerns raised during the ratification debates of the Constitution.

The intense debate between Federalists and Anti-Federalists led to the need for specific guarantees of individual freedoms and rights, as well as limitations on the government's power. The Bill of Rights amendments serve to protect fundamental personal liberties, such as freedom of speech, religion, and the press, the right to bear arms, and protection against unreasonable searches and seizures. They also ensure due process of law and the right to a fair trial by jury. Additionally, the amendments clarify that any powers not expressly granted to the federal government by the Constitution are reserved for the states or the people.

These amendments build upon the principles outlined in earlier documents, including the Virginia Declaration of Rights from 1776, which emphasized the importance of individual rights and freedoms. The Northwest Ordinance of 1787, English Bill of Rights from 1689, and even Magna Carta from 1215 also influenced the concepts found in the Bill of Rights.

By explicitly outlining these rights and limitations, the United States Bill of Rights has become a crucial part of American governance, ensuring that the government respects and protects the rights of its citizens. It has played a pivotal role in shaping the country's legal framework and remains a cornerstone of American democracy, inspiring similar declarations of rights and liberties worldwide (Bryan, 2012).

The United States Bill of Rights, consisting of the first ten amendments to the U.S. Constitution, was crafted largely due to the efforts of Representative James Madison. Madison studied the criticisms of the Constitution raised by Anti-Federalists and proposed a series of corrective measures to address these concerns. On September 25, 1789, Congress approved twelve articles of amendment, and they were submitted to the states for ratification.

Contrary to Madison's initial proposal, the amendments were not incorporated directly into the main body of the Constitution but were presented as supplemental additions. Articles Three through Twelve were ratified on December 15, 1791, becoming Amendments One through Ten of the Constitution. Article Two became the Twenty-seventh Amendment on May 5, 1992. Article One remains pending before the states and has not been ratified.

The initial amendments submitted by Madison were intended to apply only to the federal government, and they did not extend protections to the states. However, with the ratification of the Fourteenth Amendment in the 1860s, the door was opened for the application of some provisions of the Bill of Rights to state governments. This process is known as incorporation.

Since the early 20th century, both federal and state courts have used the Fourteenth Amendment to apply portions of the Bill of Rights to state and local governments, ensuring that individual rights are protected at all levels of government.

Several original engrossed copies of the Bill of Rights are still in existence, and one of them is on public display at the National Archives in Washington, D.C., where it serves as a powerful symbol of the fundamental liberties and freedoms enshrined in the United States Constitution.

Seneca Falls Declaration of Sentiments (1848)

The Seneca Falls Declaration of Sentiments is a pivotal document in the history of women's rights and the feminist movement. It was written and adopted during the Seneca Falls Convention, held in Seneca Falls, New York, on July 19-20, 1848. The convention was organized by women's rights advocates Elizabeth Cady Stanton and Lucretia Mott, among others.

The Declaration of Sentiments was modeled after the United States Declaration of Independence and is often referred to as the "Declaration of Rights and Sentiments.

"It outlined the grievances and demands of women, highlighting the lack of legal and social rights they faced in society. The document passionately argued for gender equality and women's rights as a matter of justice and human rights.

The Declaration of Sentiments began with the iconic phrase: "We hold these truths to be self-evident: that all men and women are created equal." It proceeded to list various grievances, such as women's lack of suffrage, legal inequality, and exclusion from education and professions. The document also called for an end to discriminatory marriage laws and the recognition of women's rights within the family.

One of the most significant resolutions of the declaration was the demand for women's suffrage, which became a central goal of the women's suffrage movement. The convention attendees, both men and women, signed the declaration, showing their commitment to the cause.

The Seneca Falls Declaration of Sentiments marked a significant milestone in the struggle for women's rights in the United States. It laid the groundwork for future women's rights movements and became an essential reference point for advocates fighting for gender equality. The document inspired generations of women and men to continue the fight for women's suffrage and the broader quest for women's rights in the United States and around the world.

The Seneca Falls Convention of 1848 holds significant historical importance as the first women's rights convention in the United States. It was a pivotal event that laid the foundation for the women's rights movement in the country. The convention was organized by pioneering women's rights advocates Elizabeth Cady Stanton and Lucretia Mott, along with other prominent activists.

The primary purpose of the convention was to discuss and address the social, civil, and religious rights and conditions of women. It took place over two days, from July 19th to July 20th, 1848, at the Wesleyan Chapel in Seneca Falls, New York. The convention's location was symbolic as Seneca Falls was an area known for its progressive social and religious movements.

The Seneca Falls Convention was widely publicized, attracting significant attention and participation from both men and women. During the convention, attendees discussed various issues faced by women, including their lack of legal rights, limited access to education and employment, and their exclusion from the political process. One of the most significant outcomes of the convention was the drafting and adoption of the "Declaration of Sentiments." Modeled after the U.S. Declaration of Independence, the declaration asserted that "all men and women are created equal" and listed a series of grievances and demands for women's rights. Notably, it called for women's suffrage, a demand that would become a central focus of the women's suffrage movement in the following decades.

The Seneca Falls Convention inspired similar gatherings across the country. Just two weeks later, the Rochester Women's Rights Convention was held in Rochester, New York. These conventions paved the way for the establishment of annual National Women's Rights Conventions starting in 1850. The Seneca Falls Convention marked the beginning of an organized and vocal movement for women's rights in the United States. It was a crucial step towards advancing gender equality and the fight for women's suffrage, which culminated in the passage of the 19th Amendment in 1920, granting women the right to vote. The convention remains a significant moment in the ongoing struggle for women's rights and has inspired generations of activists to continue the fight for gender equality and social justice (McMillen, 2008, p 20).

International Labour Organization (ILO) Conventions

The International Labour Organization (ILO) is a specialized agency of the United Nations with a mission to promote social and economic justice worldwide by establishing international labour standards.

It was established in October 1919 under the League of Nations and is one of the oldest agencies of the UN. Currently, the ILO has 187 member states, including 186 out of 193 UN member states and the Cook Islands. The organization is headquartered in Geneva, Switzerland, and operates approximately 40 field offices across the globe, employing around 3,381 staff members in 107 countries, with 1,698 engaged in technical cooperation programs and projects.

The main goal of the ILO is to ensure accessible, productive, and sustainable work conditions globally, emphasizing freedom, equity, security, and dignity for all workers. This objective is achieved through the establishment of international labour standards, which are outlined in 189 conventions and treaties. Among these, eight are considered fundamental according to the 1998 Declaration on Fundamental Principles and Rights at Work. These fundamental principles aim to protect and uphold the rights of workers and include freedom of association and the right to collective bargaining, the elimination of forced or compulsory labour, the abolition of child labour, and the eradication of employment and occupation discrimination.

By promoting these standards, the ILO contributes significantly to the development and implementation of international labour law, working towards a world where workers' rights are respected, and all individuals can work in fair and just conditions. The ILO's efforts are crucial in advancing social justice and improving the lives of workers and their families worldwide.

CHAPTER FOUR

Factors that Led to the Emergence of the UDHR

The Universal Declaration of Human Rights (UDHR) emerged in the aftermath of World War II and was influenced by several key factors that shaped its creation:

World War II and the Holocaust: The horrors of World War II, including the Holocaust and other widespread human rights abuses, brought global attention to the urgent need for international human rights protections. The atrocities committed during the war highlighted the consequences of unchecked state power and discrimination, motivating the international community to prevent future abuses.

Factors that Led to the Emergence of the UDHR

1. World War I and its Impact on Human Rights Discourse: World War I, which lasted from 1914 to 1918, was a devastating conflict that had a profound impact on human rights discourse. The war witnessed widespread violence, loss of life, and destruction, leading to a growing recognition of the need to protect fundamental human rights.

2. The League of Nations' Failure: The failure of the League of Nations, the precursor to the United Nations, to prevent aggression and protect human rights during the 1930s and early 1940s demonstrated the need for a more effective international organization and a comprehensive framework for safeguarding human rights.

3. Leadership of Key Figures: Influential leaders and activists, such as Eleanor Roosevelt, René Cassin, and Charles Malik, played critical roles in shaping the UDHR. Eleanor Roosevelt, as chair of the UN Human Rights Commission, was instrumental in guiding the drafting process and ensuring its adoption.

4. The UN Charter: The United Nations Charter, adopted in 1945, enshrined the commitment to promoting

human rights as one of its core principles. This commitment provided the foundation for the subsequent development of the UDHR.

5. Global Public Opinion: Public awareness and international support for human rights grew significantly in the post-war period. Civil society organizations, advocacy groups, and public opinion contributed to the demand for a comprehensive and universal declaration of human rights.

6. Multi-Cultural Collaboration: The UDHR drafting process involved contributions from individuals and experts representing various cultural, religious, and legal backgrounds. This collaboration helped ensure that the declaration reflected a broad consensus of human rights values and principles.

7. Lessons from History: The drafters of the UDHR drew inspiration from historical human rights documents, such as the Magna Carta, the English Bill of Rights, and the French Declaration of the Rights of Man and of the Citizen, recognizing the importance of building upon these past efforts.

The culmination of these factors resulted in the adoption of the UDHR by the United Nations General Assembly on December 10, 1948. The UDHR remains a landmark document, serving as a universal standard for the protection of human rights and a guiding framework for subsequent international human rights treaties and conventions.

World War I and its impact on Human rights Discourse

World War I, also known as the First World War or WWI, was a highly destructive and deadly global conflict that occurred from July 28, 1914, to November 11, 1918.

It involved two opposing coalitions, the Allies and the Central Powers, and was fought across various regions, including Europe, the Middle East, Africa, the Pacific, and parts of Asia. The war resulted in immense human suffering, with an estimated 9 million soldiers killed in combat and another 23 million wounded. Additionally, approximately 5 million civilians lost their lives due to military actions, famine, and disease. The war also contributed to other devastating events, including genocides and the 1918 Spanish flu pandemic, which was exacerbated by the movement of combatants during the conflict.

The roots of WWI can be traced back to increasing diplomatic tensions among the major European powers during the early 20th century. The assassination of Archduke Franz Ferdinand, heir to the Austro-Hungarian throne, on June 28, 1914, in Sarajevo by a Bosnian Serb named Gavrilo Princip, served as a trigger for the war. Austria-Hungary blamed Serbia for the assassination and declared war on July 28. Russia came to Serbia's defense, leading to a series of defensive alliances that drew in other major powers such as Germany, France, and Britain. The Ottoman Empire also entered the war in November, further escalating the conflict.

The outbreak of WWI was a result of complex geopolitical rivalries, nationalistic fervor, and competing imperial interests among the major powers. The war's devastating consequences had far-reaching impacts on global politics, economies, and societies, leading to significant changes in the post-war world order and setting the stage for subsequent conflicts.

The outbreak and aftermath of World War I had significant implications for human rights discourse and the emergence of the Universal Declaration of Human Rights (UDHR).

The war brought unprecedented levels of destruction and suffering, with millions of lives lost and countless others affected physically and psychologically.

The immense human cost of the war and the atrocities committed during the conflict raised international awareness about the importance of protecting and promoting human rights.

The war also exposed the shortcomings and inadequacies of existing international legal frameworks in safeguarding human rights. The formation and collapse of the League of Nations, which was established after the war as a precursor to the United Nations, highlighted the need for a more robust and effective international organization to address human rights violations and promote peace and security.

Austro-Hungary crown prince; Gavrilo Princip following his arrest.

Courtesy: Jeanette Lamb - January 11, 2017 (historycollections.com)

The League of Nations attempted to address human rights issues through the establishment of the International Labor Organization (ILO), which aimed to protect workers' rights and improve labor conditions globally.

While the ILO contributed to the advancement of social and economic justice, it also revealed the limitations of addressing human rights solely within the framework of labor rights.

The aftermath of World War I and the failure of the Treaty of Versailles to address underlying political, economic, and social issues in a comprehensive manner contributed to the rise of extremist ideologies and led to further human rights abuses during the interwar period. These developments underscored the urgent need for a universal and comprehensive document that would articulate and protect the fundamental rights and freedoms of all individuals regardless of nationality, ethnicity, or social status.

The experience of World War I and its impact on human rights discourse laid the groundwork for the eventual emergence of the UDHR in 1948. The horrors of the war served as a stark reminder of the importance of upholding human dignity, equality, and freedom, and influenced the international community's determination to create a document that would enshrine these principles in a universal and legally binding manner (Clark, 2013).

Socio-Political Impact of WWI

World War I had a profound impact on society and the collective psyche of the people involved, leaving a lasting legacy that shaped subsequent historical developments. The unprecedented rates of casualties and the immense suffering experienced during the war had far-reaching consequences:

1. Social Trauma: The scale of death and destruction caused by the war resulted in deep social trauma. Over 8 million Europeans lost their lives, and millions more were left permanently disabled. The war shattered the optimism of the "belle époque" (beautiful era) that preceded it, and the devastating impact on families and communities left a profound mark on society.

2. Birth of Extremist Ideologies: The war gave rise to extremist ideologies such as fascism and Bolshevism. The instability and disarray caused by the war paved

the way for the rise of authoritarian regimes and radical political movements in various countries, leading to further conflicts and human rights abuses.

3. Collapse of Empires: The war led to the dissolution of several major empires, including the Ottoman, Habsburg, Russian, and German Empires. This brought about significant geopolitical changes and the emergence of new nation-states in Europe and the Middle East.

4. The Lost Generation: Those who experienced the horrors of the war firsthand, especially the soldiers who fought in the trenches, were often referred to as the "Lost Generation." The war deeply affected their lives and perceptions, and many struggled with physical and psychological trauma.

5. Shell Shock and Post-Traumatic Stress Disorder: Many soldiers returned home with severe trauma, suffering from shell shock, a condition now understood as related to post-traumatic stress disorder (PTSD). The war's psychological impact on veterans and the wider society contributed to the growing mythological status of the conflict.

6. Commemoration and Mourning: In the aftermath of the war, people mourned the loss of loved ones and the many disabled. Memorials, commemorations, and remembrance rituals became an essential part of the post-war landscape.

7. Changing Historical Interpretations: The perception of World War I and its impact on society has evolved over time. Historians like Dan Todman, Paul Fussell, and Samuel Heyns have challenged common perceptions and myths surrounding the war, arguing that the experiences of individual soldiers varied widely and that not all participants shared in the same traumatic experiences.

Overall, World War I left a profound imprint on the world, shaping political, social, and cultural developments in the 20th century and beyond.

It also laid the groundwork for subsequent global conflicts and influenced the emergence of human rights movements and international organizations dedicated to preventing such devastation in the future (Todman, 2005).

Impact of WWI on Human Rights

World War I had a significant impact on human rights in various ways. While the concept of human rights was not as well-developed during that time as it is today, the war exposed numerous human rights violations and set the stage for advancements in international human rights law and advocacy. Some of the key impacts of WWI on human rights include:

1. Violations of Civil Liberties: During the war, many countries imposed strict censorship, suspended civil liberties, and suppressed dissent in the name of national security. Basic freedoms such as freedom of speech, assembly, and the press were curtailed, leading to violations of individual rights.

2. War Crimes and Atrocities: The war witnessed widespread atrocities, including summary executions, massacres, and mistreatment of prisoners of war. These actions violated the principles of humanity and established the need for accountability for war crimes.

3. Treatment of Soldiers: Soldiers endured appalling conditions in the trenches, facing brutal warfare and psychological trauma. The mistreatment of soldiers brought attention to the need for better protection of their rights and improved conditions for prisoners of war.

4. Impact on Civilians: Civilian populations suffered greatly during the war, facing hunger, displacement, and violence. The targeting of civilian populations by

both sides raised awareness of the need to protect non-combatants during armed conflicts.

5. Emergence of Humanitarian Organizations: The devastation of WWI inspired the founding of humanitarian organizations such as the International Committee of the Red Cross, which sought to provide aid and protection to civilians and soldiers alike.

6. Peace Treaties and Minority Rights: The post-war treaties, such as the Treaty of Versailles, recognized the rights of minority groups and addressed issues of national self-determination. These provisions laid the foundation for the recognition of minority rights in international law.

7. Advocacy for Disarmament: The catastrophic consequences of WWI led to calls for disarmament and limitations on weapons of war. Efforts to reduce arms and prevent future conflicts were seen as essential to safeguarding human rights.

8. League of Nations and Humanitarian Efforts: The establishment of the League of Nations, as a result of the war, sought to promote international cooperation and prevent future conflicts. The League worked on various humanitarian issues, including child labor, slavery, and trafficking.

9. Recognition of Labor Rights: The wartime labor shortages and exploitation of workers led to demands for better labor rights and working conditions. This contributed to the recognition of labor rights in the interwar period and beyond.

While WWI did not directly lead to the codification of modern human rights laws like the Universal Declaration of Human Rights (UDHR), its aftermath and the atrocities witnessed during the war set the stage for a growing understanding of the importance of human rights and the need for international cooperation to protect them. The lessons learned from WWI helped shape the development of international human rights norms and institutions in the decades that followed.

WW1 Panzerkampfwagen VI Tiger
Courtesy: Panzertruppen April 20, 2015
Formation and Collapse of the League of Nations and its Influence

The League of Nations was the world's first international organization established with the primary goal of promoting global peace. It was created on January 10, 1920, as a result of the Paris Peace Conference that followed the end of World War I. The League of Nations operated until April 20, 1946, when several of its functions and institutions were integrated into the newly formed United Nations (Christian, 1995).

The League of Nations aimed to achieve its main objectives as outlined in its Covenant. These objectives included preventing wars through collective security and disarmament, resolving international disputes through negotiation and arbitration, and addressing various global issues such as labor conditions, treatment of native populations, human trafficking, drug trafficking, arms trade, global health, prisoners of war, and the protection of minorities in Europe.

The Covenant of the League of Nations was part of the Treaty of Versailles and was signed on June 28, 1919, becoming effective on January 10, 1920, along with the rest of the Treaty. The League held its first meetings in January and November 1920, with Woodrow Wilson, the U.S. president, receiving the Nobel Peace Prize in 1919 for his instrumental role in its establishment.

September 1923: League of Nations Conference in Geneva, Switzerland.
Topical Press Agency / Getty Images

The establishment of the League of Nations marked a significant departure from the diplomatic approach of the preceding century. Unlike previous alliances and coalitions, the League of Nations did not possess its own armed force and instead relied on the military support of its member states, particularly the victorious Allies of World War I (Britain, France, Italy, and Japan) to enforce its decisions and maintain economic sanctions when necessary.

However, the Great Powers were often hesitant to take decisive actions, as imposing sanctions could also harm their own economies and interests.During the Second Italo-Ethiopian War, when the League accused Italian soldiers of attacking International Red Cross and Red Crescent medical tents, Benito Mussolini, the Italian leader, criticized the League's inability to effectively respond to such actions. He likened the League to being effective only when dealing with minor conflicts (sparrows shouting), but useless when confronted with significant challenges (eagles falling out). This highlighted the limitations and challenges faced by the League in fulfilling its mission of maintaining world peace and preventing aggression. Despite its noble intentions, the League of Nations faced difficulties in effectively addressing major international crises and conflicts, ultimately leading to its eventual dissolution in 1946 when it was replaced by the United Nations (Jahanpour, 2014).

The League of Nations had its peak membership with 58 members between September 1934 and February 1935. While it had some successes and failures in the 1920s, it ultimately proved unable to prevent the aggression of the Axis powers in the 1930s. The credibility of the League was undermined by the absence of the United States as a member, and the withdrawals of Japan, Germany, and Italy in the 1930s. The Soviet Union joined in 1934 but was later expelled in 1939 after invading Finland (Osakwe, 1972) (Pericles, 2000)

The outbreak of World War II in 1939 exposed the League's failure in achieving its primary goal of maintaining world peace, and it remained largely inactive until its eventual abolition. The League's existence lasted for 26 years before being replaced by the United Nations (UN) in 1946. The UN inherited and built upon some of the agencies and organizations founded by the League. Despite its shortcomings, modern scholarly consensus recognizes that the League made significant contributions to International affairs.

It advanced the rule of law globally, strengthened the concept of collective security, provided a platform for smaller nations to have a voice, and promoted economic stability in Central Europe during the 1920s. The League also raised awareness of various issues such as epidemics, slavery, child labor, colonial oppression, refugee crises, and working conditions through its commissions and committees. Furthermore, the League's mandate system put colonial powers under international scrutiny, paving the way for new forms of statehood (Ginneken, 2006) (Ginneken, 2006).

Professor David Kennedy sees the League as a pivotal moment in the institutionalization of international affairs, marking a departure from the pre-World War I methods of law and politics. Although the League did not achieve its ultimate goal of preventing global conflict, its legacy lies in the progress it made towards creating a more just and cooperative international order (Kennedy, 1987).

Impact of the failure of the League of Nations on human rights

The failure of the League of Nations had significant implications for human rights, particularly in the context of preventing aggression and protecting vulnerable populations. Some key impacts include:

1. Failure to Prevent Aggression: The League's inability to prevent the aggressive actions of Axis powers, such as Germany, Italy, and Japan, in the 1930s demonstrated the limitations of collective security and the

enforcement of international law. This failure allowed acts of aggression, such as the invasion of Ethiopia by Italy and the annexation of Austria by Germany, to go unchecked, leading to further destabilization and escalation of conflicts.

2. Erosion of Trust in Collective Security: The League's inability to stop acts of aggression eroded trust in collective security mechanisms and the idea that international cooperation could effectively maintain peace. This loss of faith in multilateral efforts hindered future attempts to address global crises and protect human rights through collective action.

3. Rise of Totalitarianism: The League's inability to effectively respond to the rise of totalitarian regimes contributed to the expansion of authoritarian rule and the suppression of human rights in various countries. Totalitarian regimes disregarded international norms and human rights standards, leading to widespread abuses of individual liberties and freedoms.

4. Refugee Crisis: The League's inability to prevent the displacement of populations due to conflicts and the rise of authoritarian regimes resulted in a significant refugee crisis. Millions of people were forced to flee their homes, seeking safety and asylum in other countries. The League's failure to address this crisis adequately highlighted the need for more comprehensive and effective mechanisms for protecting refugees' rights.

5. Abandonment of Minorities: The League's inability to protect the rights of minority populations in certain regions allowed for discrimination, persecution, and violence against minority groups. This failure contributed to human rights violations, particularly in the context of ethnic and religious minorities.

6. Limited Progress on Disarmament: Despite efforts to promote disarmament, the League's inability to achieve meaningful arms control measures contributed to the arms race and the militarization of certain nations. This had a negative impact on human rights, as increased military spending diverted resources from social welfare and development.

Overall, the League's failure to prevent aggression, protect vulnerable populations, and promote collective security undermined its credibility as a global peacekeeper.

The lessons learned from the League's shortcomings played a crucial role in shaping the design and approach of its successor, the United Nations, in addressing human rights challenges and promoting international cooperation for peace and security.

World War II and the urgency to establish global human rights standards

World War II had a profound impact on the urgency to establish global human rights standards. The atrocities committed during the war, including the Holocaust, the genocide of six million Jews, and other crimes against humanity, shocked the world and exposed the grave consequences of unchecked state power and discrimination.

The widespread human rights abuses during World War II highlighted the need for a comprehensive and universally recognized framework to protect the rights and dignity of individuals worldwide. The horrors of the war demonstrated that the existing legal instruments and international norms were insufficient to prevent such atrocities and hold perpetrators accountable.

As the war came to an end, the international community was determined to create an organization that would foster global cooperation and prevent future conflicts. This sense of urgency led to the establishment of the United Nations (UN) in 1945. The UN Charter proclaimed the organization's commitment to promoting and encouraging respect for human rights and fundamental freedoms for all without distinction as to race, sex, language, or religion.

In this context, the Universal Declaration of Human Rights (UDHR) emerged as a pivotal response to the atrocities of World War II. Adopted by the UN General Assembly on December 10, 1948, the UDHR is a milestone document that proclaims the inalienable rights which everyone is inherently entitled to as a human being. It sets out universal human rights standards and provides a common standard of achievement for all peoples and all nations.

The drafting of the UDHR involved contributions from individuals representing diverse cultural, religious, and legal backgrounds, ensuring that it reflected a broad consensus of human rights values. This collaborative effort was driven by the determination to prevent the recurrence of the human rights abuses witnessed during the war.

The urgency to establish global human rights standards was also evident in the subsequent development of international human rights law. In the aftermath of World War II, numerous treaties and conventions were adopted to address specific human rights issues and protect vulnerable populations. These include the Convention on the Prevention and Punishment of the Crime of Genocide, the Convention on the Elimination of All Forms of Racial Discrimination, and the Convention against Torture and Other Cruel, Inhuman or Degrading Treatment or Punishment, among others.

The impact of World War II on the establishment of global human rights standards was profound and far-reaching. It served as a powerful catalyst for creating a comprehensive system of human rights protection, centered on the principles of dignity, equality, and justice for all. The atrocities of the war remain a stark reminder of the need for vigilance in upholding human rights and the importance of collective efforts to prevent future human rights violations.

World War II

World War II had a profound impact on the urgency to establish global human rights standards. The atrocities committed during the war, including the Holocaust, the genocide of six million Jews, and other crimes against humanity, shocked the world and exposed the grave consequences of unchecked state power and discrimination.

The widespread human rights abuses during World War II highlighted the need for a comprehensive and universally recognized framework to protect the rights and dignity of individuals worldwide. The horrors of the war demonstrated that the existing legal instruments and international norms were insufficient to prevent such atrocities and hold perpetrators accountable.

As the war came to an end, the international community was determined to create an organization that would foster global cooperation and prevent future conflicts. This sense of urgency led to the establishment of the United Nations (UN) in 1945.

The UN Charter proclaimed the organization's commitment to promoting and encouraging respect for human rights and fundamental freedoms for all without distinction as to race, sex, language, or religion.

In this context, the Universal Declaration of Human Rights (UDHR) emerged as a pivotal response to the atrocities of World War II.

Adopted by the UN General Assembly on December 10, 1948, the UDHR is a milestone document that proclaims the inalienable rights which everyone is inherently entitled to as a human being. It sets out universal human rights standards and provides a common standard of achievement for all peoples and all nations.

The drafting of the UDHR involved contributions from individuals representing diverse cultural, religious, and legal backgrounds, ensuring that it reflected a broad consensus of human rights values. This collaborative effort was driven by the determination to prevent the recurrence of the human rights abuses witnessed during the war.

The urgency to establish global human rights standards was also evident in the subsequent development of international human rights law. In the aftermath of World War II, numerous treaties and conventions were adopted to address specific human rights issues and protect vulnerable populations. These include the Convention on the Prevention and Punishment of the Crime of Genocide, the Convention on the Elimination of All Forms of Racial Discrimination, and the Convention against Torture and Other Cruel, Inhuman or Degrading Treatment or Punishment, among others.

Auschwitz concentration camp, Germany
By AuthorLance Longwell, May 20, 2021

The impact of World War II on the establishment of global human rights standards was profound and far-reaching. It served as a powerful catalyst for creating a comprehensive system of human rights protection, centered on the principles of dignity, equality, and justice for all. The atrocities of the war remain a stark reminder of the need for vigilance in upholding human rights and the importance of collective efforts to prevent future human rights violations.

World War II, also known as the Second World War, was a global conflict that took place from 1939 to 1945.

It involved the vast majority of the world's countries, including all major powers, who aligned themselves into two opposing military alliances: the Allies and the Axis.

The war was characterized by the mobilization of economic, industrial, and scientific resources by the participating nations, blurring the distinction between civilian and military efforts.

World War II was a complex and multifaceted global conflict that involved various events and military campaigns across different regions. The specific starting date of the war is a matter of historical debate and interpretation, as different scholars and historians may focus on different events as the catalyst for the broader conflict. In Europe, the widely accepted starting date for World War II is 1 September 1939, when Germany, under Adolf Hitler, invaded Poland. This invasion prompted the United Kingdom and France to declare war on Germany on 3 September 1939, marking the official beginning of the war in Europe.

In the Pacific, the starting date of the war is a subject of varying viewpoints. Some consider the start of the Second Sino-Japanese War on 7 July 1937, when Japan invaded China, as the beginning of the Pacific War. Others point to earlier events, such as Japan's invasion of Manchuria on 19 September 1931, or the Battles of Khalkhin Gol fought between Japan and the forces of Mongolia and the Soviet Union from May to September 1939.

Additionally, some historians view the Spanish Civil War, which began in 1936, as a prelude to World War II, as it saw the involvement of various nations and the testing of new military strategies and technologies. Different perspectives on the starting date of World War II highlight the complex and interconnected nature of the conflict, with various events and actions contributing to the outbreak of a global war. Ultimately, the war involved multiple theaters and campaigns, with a range of factors leading to its outbreak and escalation (Weinberg, 2005).

Aircraft played a crucial role in World War II, enabling strategic bombing of population centers and the use of the only two nuclear weapons ever deployed in war.

The conflict witnessed significant technological advancements in military equipment and tactics. World War II was the deadliest conflict in history, resulting in an estimated 70 to 85 million fatalities, with civilians bearing the brunt of the casualties. The war saw widespread human suffering, including genocides, such as the Holocaust, where millions of Jews and other minorities were systematically killed by Nazi Germany. Additionally, starvation, massacres, and disease claimed the lives of millions of people (Wells, 2014).

Following the defeat of the Axis powers, Germany and Japan were occupied by Allied forces, and war crimes tribunals were conducted to hold accountable the leaders responsible for atrocities committed during the war.

The Nuremberg Trials prosecuted German officials for crimes against humanity, war crimes, and other violations of international law.

Similarly, the Tokyo Trials held Japanese leaders accountable for their actions during the war.

The aftermath of World War II led to significant geopolitical changes, with the rise of the United States and the Soviet Union as superpowers and the division of Europe into Eastern and Western blocs during the Cold War.

The devastation caused by the war prompted efforts to establish international organizations, such as the United Nations, to promote global cooperation, peace, and human rights.

German Junkers Ju-87 1941 Stock Photo – Alamy

World War II serves as a somber reminder of the immense human cost of armed conflicts and the need for international efforts to prevent future wars and safeguard human rights. It remains a pivotal event in modern history, shaping the course of the world and influencing the development of international law and institutions dedicated to preventing conflict and promoting global peace and security.
World War II was a complex and multifaceted global conflict with numerous contributing factors. While the causes are debated, several events and tensions set the stage for the outbreak of the war (Ferris and Mawdsley, 2015).

Contributing factors included the Second Italo-Ethiopian War, where Italy's invasion of Ethiopia in 1935-1936 heightened tensions and revealed the limitations of collective security and League of Nations' response. The Spanish Civil War (1936-1939) served as a testing ground for new military technologies and tactics, and also became a proxy war with involvement from other European powers. The Second Sino-Japanese War, which began in 1937, escalated into a major theater of the war, especially after Japan's aggressive actions in Asia (Förster and Gessler, 2005).

Border skirmishes between the Soviet Union and Japan in 1938-1939 further strained international relations. The rise of totalitarian regimes, particularly Nazi Germany under Adolf Hitler and Fascist Italy under Benito Mussolini, created an atmosphere of militarism and expansionism. Additionally, the unresolved issues and harsh terms imposed on Germany by the Treaty of Versailles after World War I contributed to a sense of injustice and instability in Europe.

World War II officially began on 1 September 1939 when Nazi Germany, led by Adolf Hitler, invaded Poland. In response, the United Kingdom and France declared war on Germany on 3 September. Prior to this, Germany and the Soviet Union had signed the Molotov-Ribbentrop Pact in August 1939, secretly dividing Eastern Europe and agreeing on spheres of influence (Ghuhl, 2007)

In the period from late 1939 to early 1941, Germany, in alliance with Italy, Japan, and other countries forming the Axis, launched a series of campaigns and treaties that led to the conquest or control of much of continental Europe. The war involved battles and conflicts in North Africa, East Africa, the Balkans, and the skies over Britain during the Battle of Britain and the Blitz (Polmar and Thomas, 1991).

On 22 June 1941, Germany initiated Operation Barbarossa, launching an invasion of the Soviet Union, marking the beginning of the Eastern Front. The Eastern Front became the largest land theatre of war in history, with fierce and prolonged battles between German forces and the Soviet Union. World War II continued to evolve and expand, involving numerous countries and regions in a global conflict that ultimately led to immense human suffering, loss of life, and widespread destruction. The war concluded in 1945 with the defeat of the Axis powers and the reshaping of the global political landscape (Hett etal, 1996).

World War II had a profound impact on the global political landscape and social structure, leading to significant changes in the international order and shaping the course of the 20th century and beyond. The war began with Japan's expansionist ambitions in Asia and the Pacific and escalated into a global conflict with the Axis powers (Germany, Italy, and Japan) and the Allied forces (including the United States, United Kingdom, Soviet Union, and China). The war saw major battles and offensives in various theaters, resulting in immense human suffering, loss of life, and widespread destruction.

The defeat of the Axis powers led to the reshaping of the post-war world. The United Nations was established to promote international cooperation and prevent future conflicts, with the five victorious great powers becoming permanent members of the Security Council. The Soviet Union and the United States emerged as superpowers, leading to the Cold War, a period of intense rivalry and tension between the two powers and their respective allies (Taylor 1979).

The war also triggered the decolonization of Africa and Asia, as the influence of the European great powers waned due to the devastation of their industries and economies. Many former colonies sought independence and self-determination in the post-war era.

Economically, countries affected by the war began the process of recovery and expansion. Political and economic integration efforts, particularly in Europe, aimed to foster cooperation, end pre-war enmities, and create a sense of common identity to prevent future hostilities.

World War II also had a lasting impact on human rights and the development of international law. The war atrocities, including the Holocaust, led to increased awareness and calls for the protection of human rights. The Nuremberg and Tokyo war crimes trials held accountable individuals responsible for crimes against humanity.

In summary, World War II fundamentally transformed the geopolitical landscape, leading to the establishment of new international institutions and rival superpowers, while also paving the way for decolonization, economic recovery, and efforts towards political integration and cooperation. It also brought about a renewed focus on human rights and the need for global cooperation to prevent future conflicts (Kellog William, 2003).

Impact of WWII on Human Rights and Civil Liberty

World War II had a profound impact on human rights and civil liberties, both during the conflict and in its aftermath. Here are some of the key ways in which the war affected these fundamental rights:

Casualties and War Crimes

World War II had a devastating impact on human lives, with an estimated 60 million people losing their lives during the conflict. The casualties were vast, with around 20 million military personnel and 40 million civilians perishing. These deaths were caused by various factors, including deliberate genocide, massacres, mass bombings, disease, and starvation. The Holocaust, orchestrated by the Nazi regime, resulted in the systematic killing of around 6 million Jews, as well as millions of other minorities, including Romanian people, homosexuals, ethnic Poles, and other Slavs.

The war in Asia and the Pacific, particularly involving Japanese troops, also saw large civilian casualties, with estimates ranging from 3 million to over 10 million people killed by Japanese forces.

The war witnessed horrifying atrocities, including the infamous Nanking Massacre, during which tens of thousands of Chinese civilians were raped and murdered by Japanese troops. Axis forces, including the Germans and Japanese, also used biological and chemical weapons, causing further suffering and death (Redžić, 2005).

Beyond direct military engagements, the mass bombing of cities in Europe and Asia, including the atomic bombings of Hiroshima and Nagasaki by the United States, resulted in significant civilian casualties and destruction.War crimes were committed by multiple parties during the conflict. The Soviet Union was responsible for the Katyn massacre and the imprisonment or execution of political prisoners. Soviet soldiers also committed mass rapes in occupied territories. German troops engaged in mass rapes in the Soviet Union, while there is uncertainty about the exact number of German women and girls raped by Soviet troops (Hosking, 2003).

The war crimes and atrocities committed during World War II led to the establishment of mechanisms for accountability and justice, including the Nuremberg Trials and other war crimes tribunals. It also emphasized the urgent need for international law and protections for human rights during times of conflict.The horrors of World War II and its devastating impact on human lives and rights served as a powerful impetus for the establishment of the Universal Declaration of Human Rights in 1948. The atrocities committed during the war reinforced the importance of protecting human rights and ensuring that such atrocities would never happen again. The war's aftermath marked a turning point in the global recognition of human rights as a fundamental and universal concept, leading to efforts to prevent future conflicts and protect the rights and dignity of all individuals (Obrien, 2010).

Genocide and Concentration camps

World War II witnessed some of the most egregious human rights violations in history, including genocide, concentration camps, and slave labor.

The Holocaust orchestrated by Nazi Germany resulted in the deliberate murder of approximately 6 million Jews, along with around 4 million others who were deemed "unworthy of life," including disabled individuals, mentally ill, Romani, homosexuals, Freemasons, Jehovah's Witnesses, and Soviet prisoners of war. Nazi Germany operated death camps, where people were exterminated on an industrial scale (Lieberman, 1996).

Forced labor was extensively used by Nazi Germany, with approximately 12 million Europeans from German-occupied countries abducted and used as a slave workforce in various industries and agriculture. The conditions in Nazi concentration camps and forced labor camps were brutal, leading to the death of millions (Barber and Harrison, 2006).

The Soviet Union's Gulag system also saw deadly camps during the war, with wartime privation and hunger causing numerous deaths among inmates, including foreign citizens and Axis prisoners of war. After the war, many Soviet prisoners liberated from Nazi camps were detained in special filtration camps and subjected to evaluation, with a significant number sent to the Gulag as perceived Nazi collaborators (Christofferson and Christofferson, 2006).

Japanese prisoner-of-war camps, used as labor camps, had high death rates. The treatment of Western prisoners by the Japanese was particularly harsh, resulting in a death rate seven times that of POWs under the Germans and Italians. Chinese civilians were also enslaved in large numbers for work in mines and war industries by the East Asia Development Board (Rahn, 2001).

The war crimes committed during World War II underscored the urgent need for the establishment of international human rights standards and mechanisms for accountability. The atrocities and violations of human rights witnessed during the war played a pivotal role in shaping the global consensus on the importance of upholding human rights, leading to the establishment of the Universal Declaration of Human Rights in 1948 and the subsequent development of international human rights law. The horrors of the war continue to serve as a stark reminder of the consequences of unchecked violations of human rights and the need for collective efforts to prevent such atrocities from occurring again.

Holocaust

The Holocaust, as a significant part of World War II, had a profound impact on human rights. It exemplified the extreme consequences of unchecked hatred and discrimination, and it remains one of the most significant violations of human rights in history.

1. Violation of the Right to Life: The Holocaust resulted in the mass extermination of approximately 6 million Jews and millions of other innocent individuals. It was a

clear violation of the fundamental right to life, highlighting the grave consequences when the right to life is not protected.

2. Targeting Minorities: The Holocaust targeted not only Jews but also other minority groups, including Romani people, disabled individuals, homosexuals, Jehovah's Witnesses, and others. This demonstrated the danger of persecuting and discriminating against specific groups based on their race, religion, or ethnicity.

3. Systematic Genocide: The Holocaust was a meticulously planned and systematic genocide carried out by the Nazi regime. It showed the dangers of unchecked power and the need for strong mechanisms to protect human rights and prevent such atrocities from happening in the future.

4. Failure to Protect: The Holocaust also revealed the failure of the international community to intervene and protect those at risk. Many countries closed their borders to Jewish refugees, leaving them vulnerable to persecution and death. This emphasized the importance of international cooperation and collective responsibility in safeguarding human rights.

5. Aftermath and Accountability: In the aftermath of World War II, the Nuremberg Trials held Nazi leaders accountable for their crimes, establishing the principle of individual responsibility for human rights violations. These trials set a precedent for future war crime trials and underscored the need for justice and accountability in the face of human rights abuses.

6. Holocaust Remembrance and Education: The memory of the Holocaust has since become a crucial aspect of human rights education and remembrance. It serves as a stark reminder of the consequences of prejudice and discrimination, fostering efforts to promote tolerance, understanding, and respect for all individuals.

7. Strengthening Human Rights Protections: The horrors of the Holocaust and other atrocities during World War II played a significant role in shaping the international human rights framework. They underscored the need for strong legal and institutional mechanisms to protect human rights and prevent future genocides.

In conclusion, the Holocaust and World War II had a profound and lasting impact on human rights. It exposed the darkest depths of human cruelty and the urgent need to protect and uphold the rights and dignity of all individuals, regardless of their background. The lessons learned from this tragic period continue to inform efforts to prevent human rights abuses and promote a world based on peace, justice, and respect for all.

Bengal Famine

The Bengal Famine of 1943 was one of the many devastating consequences of World War II on human rights. The war had far-reaching effects on societies and populations, leading to massive violations of basic human rights in various regions, including Bengal. The Bengal famine of 1943 was a devastating humanitarian crisis that occurred in the Bengal province of British India (now Bangladesh, West Bengal, Odisha, and eastern India) during World War II. The famine resulted in the deaths of an estimated 800,000 to 3.8 million Bengalis, out of a population of 60.3 million, due to starvation, malnutrition, diseases, and other factors aggravated by wartime disruptions, government policies, and natural disasters (O'grada, 2008).

A STARVING FAMILY, VICTIMS OF THE BENGAL FAMINE, ARRIVES IN CALCUTTA IN SEARCH OF FOOD. (PHOTO: GETTY IMAGES)

Several factors contributed to the severity of the famine. Bengal's predominantly agrarian economy struggled to cope with a rapidly growing population, leading to landlessness and chronic debt among the rural poor. Wartime inflation and wage disparities further exacerbated the situation, leaving many workers unable to afford basic food items. Additionally, disruptions in rice imports during the Japanese occupation of Burma, as well as restricted access to grain due to emergency trade barriers, worsened the food crisis.

The response from the colonial government was inadequate, with ineffective humanitarian aid and price controls that led to a black market and hyperinflation.

It was only when the British Indian Army took control of funding in October 1943 that aid increased significantly. Relief efforts were further hindered by the delayed arrival of effective aid and support. The Bengal famine of 1943 remains a subject of debate among scholars, with some attributing it to anthropogenic factors such as colonial policies and government mismanagement, while others argue that natural causes also played a significant role. Despite the challenges, the famine eventually subsided with a record rice harvest in December 1943, leading to a decline in starvation-related deaths. However, disease outbreaks in 1944 continued to claim lives, making the overall impact of the famine even more devastating.The Bengal famine of 1943 left a profound mark on the region, disintegrating families, impoverishing millions, and disrupting the social fabric of the affected areas. It stands as a tragic example of the consequences of food insecurity and the importance of effective governance and humanitarian aid during times of crisis (Arnold, 1991).

1. Impact of War on Resources: World War II disrupted global trade and resources, affecting food supplies in many parts of the world. In the case of Bengal, the war disrupted agricultural production and transportation, exacerbating food shortages. The diversion of resources to support the war effort and the prioritization of other regions over Bengal by the British colonial administration worsened the famine situation.

2. Failure of Relief Efforts: The Bengal Famine highlighted the failure of the colonial government to prioritize the lives and well-being of its citizens during a humanitarian crisis. Despite knowing the severity of the famine, the relief efforts were inadequate, and bureaucratic delays hindered the timely delivery of aid. This failure to provide essential relief and assistance during the crisis resulted in the loss of hundreds of

thousands of lives, constituting a violation of the right to life and the right to food.

3. Inequality and Discrimination: The impact of the famine was not evenly distributed, and marginalized communities were disproportionately affected. The famine's effects were particularly severe among vulnerable populations, such as the poor, marginalized ethnic groups, and marginalized religious communities. This demonstrated how wartime policies and resource distribution can exacerbate existing inequalities and lead to the violation of human rights.

4. Social and Economic Disruption: The famine resulted in massive social and economic disruption in Bengal. Families lost their livelihoods, and many were forced to migrate in search of food and work. This displacement and migration had long-lasting impacts on communities and individuals, underscoring the importance of protecting the right to live in one's homeland and the right to livelihood.

5. Legacy and Lessons Learned: The Bengal Famine serves as a stark reminder of the impact of war on human rights and the responsibility of governments to prioritize the welfare of their citizens during crises. It highlighted the need for effective governance, responsible policies, and humanitarian aid to prevent and mitigate the consequences of such disasters.

Overall, the Bengal Famine of 1943 is a tragic example of how World War II had a profound impact on human rights.
It exposed the vulnerabilities of societies during times of conflict, the importance of providing relief and assistance to affected populations, and the need to address inequalities and discrimination in resource distribution.

The lessons learned from this devastating famine have contributed to efforts to protect human rights during times of crisis and to promote policies that prioritize the welfare and well-being of all individuals, regardless of their background or circumstances.

Other Impacts of WWII on Human Rights

1. Bombings and Destruction: The war saw extensive bombings of cities, leading to massive destruction of civilian infrastructure and homes. The aerial bombardments of cities such as London, Berlin, Tokyo, and many others caused significant loss of civilian lives and heightened the urgency to protect civilians during wartime. The use of atomic bombs on Hiroshima and Nagasaki marked the first and only instances of nuclear warfare, highlighting the devastating impact of such weapons on human life and rights.

2. Displacement and Refugees: The war led to mass displacements of people, creating millions of refugees who fled their homes seeking safety. The forced migrations and disruptions of populations highlighted the need to protect the rights of refugees and ensure their safety and well-being during times of conflict.

3. Humanitarian Crises and Famine: As mentioned earlier, the Bengal Famine of 1943 was one of the humanitarian crises during the war, resulting from food shortages and inadequate relief efforts. The famine's devastating impact on human lives underscored the importance of prioritizing humanitarian aid and assistance during crises to protect the right to food and the right to life.

4. Impact on Children and Innocent Victims: World War II also had a profound impact on children and innocent civilians who suffered the consequences of war. Many children lost their families, homes, and access to education, facing long-term trauma and disruption to their development. The war's atrocities on civilians

highlighted the need to protect the rights and well-being of the most vulnerable in times of conflict.

The unprecedented scale of deaths and destruction during World War II served as a stark reminder of the importance of human rights protections during times of war and conflict. The post-war era led to the establishment of international legal frameworks, such as the Universal Declaration of Human Rights, to prevent such atrocities from happening again and to safeguard the dignity and rights of all individuals, irrespective of nationality, race, or religion. The lessons learned from World War II continue to shape efforts to promote peace, justice, and respect for human rights in the world today (Sprague and Griffiths, 2006).

World War II had a profound and lasting impact on the urgency to establish global human rights standards. The war was marked by unprecedented atrocities, including the Holocaust, where millions of Jews and other minority groups were systematically exterminated. This horrifying genocide highlighted the need for robust international protections against discrimination and persecution based on race, religion, or ethnicity.

The war also exposed widespread war crimes and violations of human rights, leading to the establishment of the Nuremberg Trials and other post-war tribunals. These trials emphasized individual accountability for human rights violations, setting a precedent for future war crime trials and reinforcing the principle that those responsible for gross abuses of human rights should be held accountable.

The displacement and refugee crisis resulting from World War II further underscored the importance of upholding the rights of individuals fleeing conflict and persecution. The world witnessed the plight of millions of displaced people, necessitating the need for strong protections for refugees and humanitarian assistance to those in need.

The extensive destruction of cities and civilian infrastructure during the war demonstrated the urgency of safeguarding civilians during armed conflicts. The targeting of civilian populations and indiscriminate bombings highlighted the need for measures to protect civilians from harm and uphold their fundamental rights.

Humanitarian crises, such as the Bengal Famine of 1943, further emphasized the vulnerabilities of populations during times of conflict and underscored the importance of providing humanitarian aid and assistance to those facing dire circumstances.

The urgency to establish global human rights standards also stemmed from the desire for increased global cooperation and peacekeeping efforts to prevent future conflicts. The establishment of the United Nations (UN) in 1945 aimed to foster international cooperation and maintain world peace, with the goal of preventing future wars and human rights violations.

Advocacy and awareness for human rights significantly increased in the aftermath of World War II. Civil society organizations, activists, and survivors played a crucial role in advocating for the establishment of global human rights standards. Their voices, combined with the collective horror of the war's atrocities, contributed to the drafting and adoption of the Universal Declaration of Human Rights (UDHR) in 1948.

The UDHR laid the foundation for international human rights law, enshrining a comprehensive set of rights and freedoms that all individuals are entitled to, regardless of their nationality, race, or religion. It was a landmark achievement in the recognition and protection of human rights on a global scale.

In conclusion, the urgency to establish global human rights standards after World War II was fueled by the desire to prevent future atrocities, promote peace and justice, and create a world where human rights are protected and upheld for every person. The lessons learned from the war continue to shape the international human rights framework, reminding the world of the importance of preventing discrimination, upholding individual accountability, and fostering cooperation to create a more just and equitable world.

Formation of the United Nations in 1945 and its role in human rights

The formation of the United Nations (UN) was a direct response to the devastation and human suffering caused by World War II. As the war was coming to an end in 1945, leaders from various nations recognized the urgent need for a new international organization that could promote peace, security, and cooperation among nations to prevent future conflicts and ensure a more stable world order. The concept of the United Nations was first discussed during the war. On January 1, 1942, representatives from 26 Allied nations met in Washington, D.C., and issued the Declaration by United Nations, pledging their support for the war effort against the Axis powers. This early cooperation laid the groundwork for the formation of a post-war international organization.

UN Secretariat Building Nov 20, 2005 | Photo Collections
New York, October/November 2005

In April 1945, as the war was nearing its conclusion, representatives from 50 nations gathered in San Francisco for the United Nations Conference on International Organization. The conference was held from April 25 to June 26, 1945, and its primary goal was to draft the Charter of the United Nations.

The Charter of the United Nations established the purposes, structure, and framework of the organization. It was drafted through extensive negotiations and discussions among the participating nations. Key figures, including leaders and diplomats from various countries, played critical roles in shaping the Charter.

The Charter was formally adopted and signed on June 26, 1945, by the representatives of 50 countries, officially establishing the United Nations. Among the signatories were the five permanent members of the Security Council: China, France, the Soviet Union, the United Kingdom, and the United States.

The Charter entered into force on October 24, 1945, after being ratified by the five permanent members of the Security Council and a majority of the other signatory nations. This date is now celebrated annually as United Nations Day.

The United Nations was designed to be a global organization that would serve as a platform for dialogue, cooperation, and collective action among nations. Its main purposes, as stated in the Charter, include maintaining international peace and security, promoting friendly relations among countries, fostering economic and social progress, protecting human rights, and providing a forum for addressing global issues and challenges.

Since its establishment, the United Nations has evolved and expanded its activities to address a wide range of global issues, including peacekeeping, conflict resolution, humanitarian assistance, sustainable development, environmental protection, and the promotion of human rights and fundamental freedoms. It has become a crucial international institution that aims to foster cooperation and multilateralism to tackle the complex challenges facing the world today.

The formation of the United Nations (UN) in 1945 marked a significant milestone in the history of human rights. The UN was established with the primary goal of promoting international cooperation and preventing future conflicts that could lead to the devastation witnessed during World War II. One of the fundamental principles enshrined in the UN Charter was the commitment to uphold human rights and fundamental freedoms for all people.

Role of the UN in Human Rights

Universal Declaration of Human Rights (UDHR): In the aftermath of World War II, the UN recognized the need for a universal standard of human rights to ensure the protection and dignity of individuals worldwide.

The UN General Assembly adopted the UDHR on December 10, 1948.

The UDHR is a landmark document that lays down the fundamental rights and freedoms to which every human being is entitled, regardless of their nationality, race, religion, or any other status. It serves as a common standard of achievement for all nations and has been the basis for subsequent human rights instruments.

1. International Human Rights Treaties: Building on the principles of the UDHR, the UN has worked to develop and promote a comprehensive framework of international human rights law. Over the years, numerous human rights treaties and conventions have been adopted under the auspices of the UN. These treaties address specific areas of human rights, such as civil and political rights, economic, social, and cultural rights, the rights of women, children, persons with disabilities, and more. States that become parties to these treaties commit to upholding and protecting the rights enshrined within them.

2. Human Rights Council: The UN Human Rights Council is an intergovernmental body responsible for promoting and protecting human rights around the world. It replaced the former UN Commission on Human Rights in 2006 and is composed of 47 member states elected by the UN General Assembly. The Human Rights Council reviews and addresses human rights situations in different countries, undertakes fact-finding missions, and issues resolutions and recommendations to address human rights violations.

3. Peacekeeping and Conflict Resolution: The UN plays a crucial role in peacekeeping operations and conflict resolution, aiming to prevent and mitigate armed conflicts that often lead to grave human rights abuses. Peacekeeping missions often focus on protecting civilians, ensuring human rights are respected, and facilitating post-conflict reconciliation and justice.

4. Humanitarian Assistance: The UN provides critical humanitarian assistance in times of crisis and disaster. It helps address the immediate needs of affected populations, including access to food, clean water, shelter, and medical care, all of which are essential aspects of human rights.
5. Special Procedures and Mechanisms: The UN appoints special rapporteurs and establishes expert mechanisms to monitor and report on specific human rights issues or country situations. These experts conduct fact-finding missions, investigate human rights violations, and provide recommendations for action.

Overall, the United Nations has played a central role in advancing the concept of human rights and promoting their universality, indivisibility, and interdependence. While challenges remain in fully implementing human rights protections globally, the UN continues to work towards a world where every individual's human rights are respected, protected, and fulfilled.

Leadership of Key Figures in the Formation of the UDHR

Indeed, the leadership and contributions of key figures played a crucial role in shaping the Universal Declaration of Human Rights (UDHR). Here are some influential leaders and activists who made significant contributions:

1. Eleanor Roosevelt: As the chair of the United Nations Human Rights Commission (later the Commission on Human Rights), Eleanor Roosevelt played a pivotal role in guiding the drafting process of the UDHR. She was a strong advocate for human rights and used her position to ensure that the Declaration addressed a wide range of rights and freedoms. Her leadership and diplomatic skills were instrumental in garnering support from various countries and overcoming challenges during the drafting process.

2. René Cassin: René Cassin, a French jurist and diplomat, made significant contributions to the development of the UDHR. He was one of the principal drafters of the Declaration and played a key role in synthesizing the inputs from various experts and countries. His expertise in international law and commitment to human rights principles were instrumental in shaping the language and content of the UDHR.

3. Charles Malik: Charles Malik, a Lebanese philosopher and diplomat, was another influential figure in the drafting process of the UDHR. He served as the rapporteur of the Human Rights Commission and played a crucial role in ensuring that the Declaration upheld the principles of human dignity, equality, and freedom. Malik's intellectual contributions and advocacy for human rights made a lasting impact on the final text of the UDHR.

4. John Peters Humphrey: John Peters Humphrey, a Canadian legal scholar, was the principal author of the first draft of the UDHR. He worked closely with Eleanor Roosevelt and other members of the Human Rights Commission to develop the initial framework of the Declaration. Humphrey's expertise in international law and commitment to human rights were instrumental in shaping the early stages of the UDHR.

These leaders, along with many others from different countries and backgrounds, worked tirelessly to create a comprehensive and universal document that would set forth the fundamental rights and freedoms to which all human beings are entitled. Their vision and dedication laid the foundation for the UDHR, which continues to be a fundamental instrument in the protection and promotion of human rights worldwide.

The UN Charter

The United Nations Charter is the foundational treaty of the United Nations (UN), an international organization established to promote international cooperation, maintain peace and security, and advance economic and social progress. It was signed on June 26, 1945, in San Francisco, and came into effect on October 24, 1945, after being ratified by the five permanent members of the UN Security Council and a majority of the original 51 signatory countries.

The Charter of the United Nations is the primary and fundamental treaty of the United Nations, an intergovernmental organization. It serves as the basis for the establishment of the UN system, defining its main objectives, organizational structure, and overall framework. The Charter outlines the roles and responsibilities of its six principal organs, which are the Secretariat, the General Assembly, the Security Council, the Economic and Social Council, the International Court of Justice, and the Trusteeship Council.

The UN Charter sets forth the fundamental principles and objectives of the United Nations and its member states. It mandates the UN to work towards maintaining international peace and security, upholding international law, and promoting cooperation among nations to address various challenges. These challenges include improving living standards, addressing economic, social, health, and related issues, and ensuring universal respect for human rights and fundamental freedoms for all individuals, regardless of race, sex, language, or religion. As a charter and constituent treaty, the rules and obligations outlined in the UN Charter are binding on all member states and take precedence over other treaties (Christopher, 2017).

During the Second World War, the Allied nations, known as the United Nations at that time, expressed their intention to establish a new international organization after the war.

As a result, the United Nations Charter was extensively discussed, prepared, and drafted during the San Francisco Conference that commenced on 25 April 1945. This conference involved the participation of the majority of the world's sovereign nations. After obtaining two-thirds approval from each participating nation, the final text of the UN Charter was unanimously adopted by the delegates and made available for signature on 26 June 1945. The signing ceremony took place in San Francisco, United States, and 50 of the original 51 member countries signed the Charter.

The UN Charter officially came into force on 24 October 1945, following the ratification by the five permanent members of the United Nations Security Council, which include China, France, the Soviet Union (now represented by Russia), the United Kingdom, and the United States. Additionally, a majority of the other signatory countries also ratified the Charter. This date is considered the official establishment of the United Nations. The first session of the General Assembly, representing all 51 initial member countries, was held in London the following January.

In recognition of this significant date, the General Assembly formally designated 24 October as United Nations Day in 1947, and in 1971, it was declared an official international holiday. Over time, the majority of countries, totaling 193 parties, have now ratified and become parties to the Charter, affirming their commitment to the principles and objectives of the United Nations.

Key features of the UN Charter

1. Preamble: The Preamble of the UN Charter sets out the broad goals and principles of the organization, including maintaining international peace and security, promoting respect for human rights, and encouraging social progress and better standards of living.

2. Purposes and Principles: The Charter outlines the main purposes of the UN, which include preventing war, settling disputes peacefully, and fostering friendly

relations among nations. It also sets forth key principles such as sovereign equality of member states, non-interference in domestic affairs, and respect for human rights.

3. Structure: The UN Charter establishes the principal organs of the organization, including the General Assembly, the Security Council, the Economic and Social Council, the Secretariat, the International Court of Justice, and other specialized agencies and programs.

4. Peace and Security: The Charter grants the Security Council primary responsibility for maintaining international peace and security. It authorizes the use of collective measures, including economic sanctions and military actions, to address threats to peace and acts of aggression.

5. Human Rights: While the Charter does not include a detailed enumeration of human rights, it reaffirms faith in fundamental human rights and dignity and calls for promoting and encouraging respect for human rights and fundamental freedoms for all without distinction of race, sex, language, or religion.

6. International Law: The UN Charter emphasizes the importance of settling disputes peacefully and upholding the principles of international law. It provides a framework for the peaceful resolution of conflicts and encourages states to seek solutions through negotiation and mediation.

7. Membership and Admission: The Charter outlines the procedures for membership in the UN and the criteria for admission of new member states.

8. Amendments: The Charter can be amended through a process that involves approval by two-thirds of the UN General Assembly and ratification by two-thirds of member states, including all permanent members of the Security Council.

The UN Charter remains a foundational document of international relations, guiding the work of the United Nations and serving as a framework for global cooperation, conflict resolution, and the promotion of human rights and sustainable development.

Global Public Opinion

The emergence of the Universal Declaration of Human Rights (UDHR) was significantly influenced by global opinion and the collective efforts of various individuals, organizations, and governments around the world. Here are some key factors that contributed to its creation:

1. World War II and its aftermath: The devastation and atrocities witnessed during World War II underscored the urgent need for a global commitment to human rights and peace. The war's impact highlighted the importance of respecting the dignity and rights of all individuals, regardless of their nationality, ethnicity, or religion.

2. Public outcry and advocacy: Human rights activists, organizations, and concerned citizens across the world vocally expressed their demands for an international agreement on human rights. Grassroots movements, demonstrations, and petitions played a crucial role in raising awareness about the need for universal human rights standards.

3. United Nations formation: The United Nations was established in 1945, with one of its primary goals being to promote international cooperation and protect human rights. The UN provided a platform for discussions and negotiations to create a comprehensive human rights document.

4. Leadership of key figures: Influential leaders and activists, such as Eleanor Roosevelt, René Cassin, and Charles Malik, played critical roles in shaping the UDHR. Eleanor Roosevelt, as chair of the UN Human

Rights Commission, was instrumental in guiding the drafting process and ensuring its adoption.

5. International collaboration: Delegates from various countries worked together to draft the UDHR. Different perspectives and experiences from around the world were considered to ensure that the declaration would be truly universal and applicable to all nations.

6. Post-war vision for a better world: The aftermath of World War II led many to envision a more just and peaceful world. The UDHR was seen as a concrete step towards preventing future conflicts and promoting a world where human rights were respected and protected.

7. Common moral values: Despite cultural, political, and religious differences, there was a shared recognition of certain fundamental moral values that should be upheld universally. The UDHR sought to codify these principles into a comprehensive document.

8. Impact of historical human rights declarations: The UDHR built upon earlier human rights declarations and conventions, such as the United States Bill of Rights and the Declaration of the Rights of Man and of the Citizen during the French Revolution. These documents provided a foundation and inspiration for the UDHR.

In summary, the emergence of the Universal Declaration of Human Rights was the result of a collective effort driven by global opinion, public outcry, leadership, international collaboration, and the shared vision for a world where human rights are protected and respected for all.

Multi-Cultural Collaboration

The emergence of the Universal Declaration of Human Rights (UDHR) was influenced by several significant factors and events.

The devastating impact of World War II highlighted the urgent need to prevent future conflicts and promote global cooperation. The horrors of the war, including mass atrocities and human rights abuses, underscored the importance of protecting individual dignity and ensuring fundamental human rights.

Worldwide efforts to rebuild after the war created an atmosphere of collaboration and a recognition of the interdependence of nations. Leaders from different countries saw the necessity of establishing an international organization to address global issues and foster cooperation among nations. The Charter of the United Nations, which was adopted in 1945, laid the foundation for the UDHR. It emphasized the promotion of human rights as a key principle of the UN and set the stage for the subsequent drafting of the declaration.

The UN's Commission on Human Rights, led by influential figures like Eleanor Roosevelt, played a critical role in guiding the drafting process. Representatives from various cultural, religious, and legal backgrounds collaborated to ensure that the UDHR would reflect universal values and principles while respecting the diversity of human experiences and perspectives.

The UDHR drafting process involved extensive discussions, negotiations, and compromises among member states to find common ground on human rights principles. The document was deliberately crafted to be inclusive, accessible, and applicable to people from different cultural and legal traditions.

Public engagement and input from civil society organizations and human rights activists also shaped the UDHR. Regional consultations and feedback from communities around the world helped ensure that the declaration addressed the needs and aspirations of people at the grassroots level.

The UDHR's adoption on December 10, 1948, marked a significant milestone in the history of human rights.

It represented a shared commitment by the international community to uphold the dignity and rights of every individual, regardless of their race, religion, gender, or nationality.

In conclusion, the emergence of the UDHR was the result of a complex and collaborative process, influenced by the aftermath of World War II, the establishment of the United Nations, and the collective efforts of leaders, experts, and activists from diverse backgrounds. The declaration remains a foundational document that continues to shape the global discourse on human rights and serves as a beacon of hope for a more just and equitable world.

Lessons from History

The drafting process of the Universal Declaration of Human Rights (UDHR) was a multi-cultural collaboration that brought together individuals and experts from diverse cultural, religious, and legal backgrounds. This collaboration was essential in shaping the UDHR to be a document that reflected a broad consensus of human rights values and principles.

The involvement of representatives from different countries and regions allowed for the consideration of various perspectives and experiences. Each participant brought their unique insights and understanding of human rights issues based on their cultural and historical context. This inclusivity helped to ensure that the UDHR addressed a wide range of concerns and challenges faced by people across the globe.

The diverse religious backgrounds of the participants also played a role in shaping the declaration. Many religious traditions have principles and teachings that align with human rights values, such as dignity, equality, and compassion. Incorporating these values into the UDHR contributed to its universal appeal and recognition.

Moreover, legal experts from various legal systems and traditions participated in the drafting process.

Their input was crucial in crafting language that could be interpreted and applied in different legal frameworks around the world. The drafting committee carefully considered different legal concepts and terminologies to create a document that could be understood and embraced by different legal systems.

This multi-cultural collaboration promoted empathy and understanding among the participants, fostering a sense of shared responsibility for creating a comprehensive human rights framework. It also allowed for the identification of potential cultural sensitivities or discrepancies in the interpretation of certain rights, which were addressed through constructive dialogue and negotiation.

The emphasis on collaboration and consensus-building during the drafting process helped to overcome potential divisions and ensured that the UDHR was not dominated by the interests of any particular group or region. Instead, it became a truly universal document, representing a collective commitment to protecting and promoting the rights and dignity of all individuals, regardless of their background or nationality.

In conclusion, the multi-cultural collaboration during the drafting of the UDHR brought together diverse perspectives, religious values, and legal expertise, resulting in a document that reflects a broad consensus of human rights principles. This inclusive approach has contributed to the enduring significance and universality of the UDHR as a foundational instrument in the protection of human rights worldwide.

Eleanor roosevelt holds a poster of the universal declaration of human rights. (©un photo archives)

The Universal Declaration of Human Rights (UDHR)

The Universal Declaration of Human Rights (UDHR) is a landmark international document that sets out the fundamental rights and freedoms that all individuals are entitled to, regardless of their nationality, race, religion, or any other status. It was adopted by the United Nations General Assembly on 10 December 1948 and is considered a foundational text in the field of human rights.The drafting of the UDHR was a collaborative effort involving representatives from various cultural, religious, and legal backgrounds, ensuring that the declaration reflected a broad consensus of human rights values and principles. Eleanor Roosevelt, as the chair of the UN Human Rights Commission, played a critical role in guiding the drafting process and ensuring its adoption.

The UDHR consists of 30 articles that cover a wide range of human rights, including the right to life, liberty, and security; freedom of thought, expression, and religion; protection against torture and slavery; the right to work, education, and social security; and the right to participate in government and cultural life. It embodies the principle that all human beings are born free and equal in dignity and rights.The adoption of the UDHR was a response to the atrocities of World War II, including the Holocaust and other gross violations of human rights during the war. The international community recognized the need to prevent such atrocities from happening again and to establish a common understanding of the inalienable rights that belong to every human being.

The unanimous adoption of the UDHR by the UN General Assembly demonstrated the commitment of the international community to upholding human rights and promoting peace and justice.

It signified a collective determination to protect individuals from discrimination, persecution, and abuse and to create a world where human rights are respected and upheld.

Since its adoption, the UDHR has served as a source of inspiration for the development of international human rights law and numerous national constitutions and laws. It has influenced the creation of other human rights treaties and conventions, further strengthening the protection of human rights worldwide. The UDHR is not a legally binding treaty, but it holds immense moral and political significance. It has been widely recognized as a common standard of achievement for all peoples and nations and has become a powerful tool for advocacy and human rights education. In conclusion, the Universal Declaration of Human Rights is a pivotal document that arose from the aftermath of World War II. It reflects the international community's commitment to promoting and protecting the inherent dignity and rights of every individual, regardless of their background. The UDHR continues to shape the global human rights framework, serving as a reminder of the shared responsibility to uphold and promote human rights for all (UBISNET, 2019).

The Universal Declaration of Human Rights (UDHR) is a landmark document in the history of human and civil rights. It consists of 30 articles that outline the "basic rights and fundamental freedoms" inherent to all human beings.

The declaration emphasizes the universal character of these rights, stating that they are inalienable and applicable to all individuals, regardless of their nationality, race, religion, or any other status.

Adopted as a "common standard of achievement for all peoples and all nations," the UDHR enshrines the principle that all human beings are born free and equal in dignity and rights. It serves as a moral and political commitment by nations to recognize and uphold the rights of all individuals, without discrimination.

One of the remarkable features of the UDHR is its "universalist language," which avoids specific references to any particular culture, political system, or religion.

This approach ensures that the principles and values outlined in the declaration are accessible and applicable to people from diverse backgrounds and societies.

The UDHR has been instrumental in shaping international human rights law. It directly influenced the development of the International Bill of Human Rights, which includes the International Covenant on Civil and Political Rights and the International Covenant on Economic, Social, and Cultural Rights, both completed in 1966 and in force since 1976. While the UDHR itself is not legally binding, its principles have been elaborated and incorporated into subsequent international treaties, regional human rights instruments, and national constitutions and legal codes.The declaration has served as a cornerstone of human rights advocacy and education worldwide. Its universal and aspirational nature has inspired individuals, organizations, and governments to promote and protect human rights for all. It has been a driving force behind efforts to combat discrimination, inequality, and abuses of human rights around the world. Overall, the Universal Declaration of Human Rights remains a significant milestone in the advancement of human rights and a testament to the shared values and responsibilities of the international community in upholding the dignity and rights of every individual. It continues to be a guiding document that shapes the pursuit of justice, equality, and respect for human rights globally (UN foundation, 2021).

Indeed, the Universal Declaration of Human Rights (UDHR) has had a profound impact on the development of international human rights law and its influence extends to both global and national levels.

While the UDHR itself is not legally binding, its principles and provisions have been incorporated into several binding international treaties.

There are nine core human rights treaties that have been influenced by the Declaration, covering various aspects of human rights such as civil, political, economic, social, and cultural rights. All 193 member states of the United Nations have ratified at least one of these treaties, with the majority ratifying four or more, demonstrating widespread acceptance of the principles enshrined in the UDHR.

Although the UDHR is not formally part of customary international law, it is widely recognized that many of its provisions have passed into customary international law. This means that certain rights and principles articulated in the declaration are considered legally binding on states, even if they have not ratified the relevant treaties. As a result, the UDHR has served as a foundation for the development of human rights norms and standards worldwide (Henry and Philip, 2000).

While courts in some nations have been more cautious in recognizing the legal effect of the UDHR, its broader impact on legal, political, and social developments cannot be denied. Many countries have incorporated the principles of the UDHR into their national constitutions, legal systems, and policies. It has influenced the creation of national human rights institutions and advocacy for human rights protection at the domestic level. Beyond its legal significance, the UDHR's moral and ethical force has been instrumental in promoting human rights awareness and advocacy globally. Its profound impact is reflected in its widespread recognition and acceptance, with the document being translated into 530 languages, making it the most translated document in history. This exemplifies its relevance and resonance across diverse cultures and societies (Posner, 2014).

Overall, the UDHR's enduring legacy lies in its contribution to the development of international human rights law and its role as a catalyst for positive changes in protecting and promoting human rights worldwide.

It continues to be a guiding document that inspires individuals, governments, and organizations to work towards the realization of a world where all individuals can enjoy their inherent rights and freedoms.

Structure and Content of the UDHR

The Universal Declaration of Human Rights (UDHR) is a comprehensive document consisting of a preamble and 30 articles. It was drafted by representatives from different cultural, religious, and legal backgrounds, ensuring a broad consensus on the rights and freedoms it enshrines. The structure and content of the UDHR reflect its Universalist approach, addressing the fundamental rights and dignity of all human beings.

Preamble: The preamble serves as an introductory statement that sets the tone and purpose of the declaration. It emphasizes the recognition of the inherent dignity and equal rights of all members of the human family and the importance of promoting social progress, better standards of life, and freedom from fear and want.

Articles: The UDHR consists of 30 articles that detail specific human rights and fundamental freedoms. The articles cover a wide range of rights, encompassing civil, political, economic, social, and cultural rights. Some of the key provisions include:

Article 1: All human beings are born free and equal in dignity and rights.

Article 2: Everyone is entitled to all the rights and freedoms set forth in the declaration without distinction of any kind.

Article 3: Everyone has the right to life, liberty, and security of person.

Article 5: No one shall be subjected to torture, cruel, inhuman, or degrading treatment or punishment.

Article 13: Everyone has the right to freedom of movement and residence within the borders of each state.

Article 23: Everyone has the right to work, to free choice of employment, to just and favorable conditions of work, and to protection against unemployment.

Article 25: Everyone has the right to a standard of living adequate for the health and well-being of themselves and their family, including food, clothing, housing, and medical care.

The articles emphasize the indivisibility and interdependence of human rights, underscoring that civil and political rights are inseparable from economic, social, and cultural rights.

1. Universal Character: The UDHR's content is universal in nature, deliberately avoiding references to specific cultures, political systems, or religions. It recognizes that human rights are inherent to all individuals, regardless of their nationality, race, religion, gender, or any other status. It proclaims that human rights apply to every person, everywhere, and at all times.

2. Non-Binding Nature: While the UDHR is not a legally binding treaty, it is considered a "common standard of achievement for all peoples and all nations." It reflects the moral and ethical principles that guide the international community in promoting and protecting human rights.

The structure and content of the UDHR have been influential in shaping subsequent international human rights treaties and national constitutions. Its broad and inclusive approach to human rights has been instrumental in fostering a global consensus on the importance of safeguarding the dignity and rights of every individual.

Background to the Formation of the UDHR

During World War II, the Allied nations, formally known as the United Nations, embraced the Four Freedoms as their fundamental war aims.

These Four Freedoms included freedom of speech, freedom of religion, freedom from fear, and freedom from want. These principles were seen as essential to promoting a just and peaceful world order.

As the war came to an end, the United Nations Charter was developed to reaffirm the commitment to fundamental human rights and the dignity of every individual. The Charter aimed to foster "universal respect for, and observance of, human rights and fundamental freedoms for all without distinction as to race, sex, language, or religion." It recognized the importance of upholding human rights as a means to prevent future conflicts and ensure global stability.

The revelation of the atrocities committed by Nazi Germany during the war shocked the world and highlighted the need for a more comprehensive definition of human rights. It was clear that the UN Charter, while advocating for human rights, did not provide specific details regarding the rights of individuals. To address this, there was a consensus within the international community to create a universal declaration that would spell out the rights to which every person is entitled.

Thus, the Universal Declaration of Human Rights (UDHR) was drafted, emphasizing the importance of individual rights and freedoms. The UDHR was intended to complement and give effect to the principles outlined in the UN Charter. It became a landmark document that detailed the fundamental rights and freedoms that every human being should enjoy, regardless of their background or status.

The horrors of World War II and the Holocaust played a significant role in shaping the urgent need for a universal declaration of human rights.

The atrocities committed during the war underscored the dangers of unchecked power and the disregard for human dignity and rights.

The UDHR aimed to prevent such tragedies from happening again and serve as a guiding framework for promoting human rights and fostering a more just and equitable world for all (UDHR.ORG).

Overview of the UDHR and its 30 Articles

The Universal Declaration of Human Rights (UDHR) is a historic document adopted by the United Nations General Assembly on December 10, 1948, as Resolution 217.

It is considered a foundational text in the history of human rights and serves as a common standard of achievement for all nations. The UDHR consists of 30 articles that detail the fundamental rights and freedoms to which all human beings are entitled.

Preamble

The Preamble of the Universal Declaration of Human Rights (UDHR) sets the tone and context for the document, highlighting its significance and purpose. It begins by acknowledging that recognition of the inherent dignity and equal rights of all individuals is essential for promoting freedom, justice, and peace in the world. The Preamble acknowledges the historical context of human rights abuses that have resulted in acts of barbarity, which have outraged humanity. It asserts that the highest aspiration of humanity is to create a world where people can enjoy freedom of speech, belief, and freedom from fear and want. The Preamble emphasizes the importance of protecting human rights through the rule of law to prevent resorting to rebellion against tyranny and oppression. It also recognizes the need to foster friendly relations between nations.

The Preamble refers to the United Nations Charter, where the peoples of the United Nations reaffirmed their faith in fundamental human rights and the dignity and worth of every individual.

It also expresses the commitment to promoting social progress and better standards of life in larger freedom. The document emphasizes the pledge of Member States to work together with the United Nations to promote universal respect for and observance of human rights and fundamental freedoms.

The Preamble stresses the significance of having a common understanding of human rights and freedoms to fully realize the pledge made by Member States.

Finally, the Preamble proclaims the Universal Declaration of Human Rights as a common standard of achievement for all peoples and nations.

It calls upon individuals and all sections of society to constantly keep the Declaration in mind and strive to promote respect for human rights through education and progressive measures, both nationally and internationally. The ultimate goal is to secure the universal and effective recognition and observance of human rights among all people, regardless of their nationality or jurisdiction.

Below is an overview of its key articles:

Article 1: All human beings are born free and equal in dignity and rights. They are endowed with reason and conscience and should act towards one another in a spirit of brotherhood.

Article 2: Everyone is entitled to all the rights and freedoms set forth in the Declaration, without distinction of any kind, such as race, color, sex, language, religion, political or other opinion, national or social origin, property, birth, or other status.

Article 3: Everyone has the right to life, liberty, and security of person.

Article 4: No one shall be held in slavery or servitude; slavery and the slave trade shall be prohibited in all their forms.

Article 5: No one shall be subjected to torture or to cruel, inhuman, or degrading treatment or punishment.

Article 6: Everyone has the right to recognition everywhere as a person before the law.

Article 7: All are equal before the law and are entitled without any discrimination to equal protection of the law.

Article 8: Everyone has the right to an effective remedy by the competent national tribunals for acts violating the fundamental rights granted him by the constitution or by law.

Article 9: No one shall be subjected to arbitrary arrest, detention, or exile.

Article 10: Everyone is entitled in full equality to a fair and public hearing by an independent and impartial tribunal.

Article 11: (1) Everyone charged with a penal offense has the right to be presumed innocent until proved guilty according to law.

Article 12: No one shall be subjected to arbitrary interference with his privacy, family, home, or correspondence.

Article 13: (1) Everyone has the right to freedom of movement and residence within the borders of each state.

Article 14: (1) Everyone has the right to seek and to enjoy in other countries asylum from persecution.

Article 15: (1) Everyone has the right to a nationality.

Article 16: (1) Men and women of full age, without any limitation due to race, nationality, or religion, have the right to marry and to found a family.

Article 17: (1) Everyone has the right to own property alone as well as in association with others.

Article 18: Everyone has the right to freedom of thought, conscience, and religion.

Article 19: Everyone has the right to freedom of opinion and expression.

Article 20: (1) Everyone has the right to freedom of peaceful assembly and association.

Article 21: (1) Everyone has the right to take part in the government of his country, directly or through freely chosen representatives.

Article 22: (1) Everyone, as a member of society, has the right to social security.

Article 23: (1) Everyone has the right to work, to free choice of employment, to just and favorable conditions of work.

Article 24: Everyone has the right to rest and leisure, including reasonable limitation of working hours and periodic holidays with pay.

Article 25: (1) Everyone has the right to a standard of living adequate for the health and well-being of himself and of his family.

Article 26: (1) Everyone has the right to education.

Article 27: (1) Everyone has the right freely to participate in the cultural life of the community.

Article 28: Everyone is entitled to a social and international order in which the rights and freedoms set forth in this Declaration can be fully realized.

Article 29: (1) Everyone has duties to the community in which alone the free and full development of his personality is possible.

Article 30: Nothing in this Declaration may be interpreted as implying for any State, group, or person any right to engage in any activity or to perform any act aimed at the destruction of any of the rights and freedoms set forth herein.

The UDHR has served as a foundation for subsequent international human rights treaties and continues to be a cornerstone of global efforts to promote and protect human rights for all (Glendon, 2002).

The drafting process of the UDHR

The drafting process of the Universal Declaration of Human Rights (UDHR) was a significant undertaking that involved representatives from various countries and backgrounds. It took place over two years, from 1946 to 1948, and was led by the Commission on Human Rights (CHR), a standing body within the United Nations responsible for promoting human rights.

The process began in June 1946 when the Economic and Social Council (ECOSOC) created the CHR to prepare what was initially conceived as an International Bill of Rights. The CHR consisted of 18 members from different nations, ensuring representation from various regions of the world.

The drafting committee responsible for writing the articles of the UDHR was established in February 1947.

It was chaired by Eleanor Roosevelt, the former First Lady of the United States and a prominent human rights advocate. Her leadership was crucial in guiding the committee towards a successful outcome. John Peters Humphrey, a Canadian jurist and diplomat, was appointed as the principal drafter of the Declaration.

He played a key role in shaping the content of the UDHR and translating the ideas of the committee into concrete language (Morsink, 1999).

The Drafting Committee included other notable members such as P.C. Chang of the Republic of China, René Cassin of France, and Charles Malik of Lebanon.

Their diverse expertise and perspectives enriched the discussions and ensured that the Declaration addressed the concerns and aspirations of different cultures and societies. Throughout the drafting process, the committee faced challenges in reconciling differing viewpoints and striking a balance between the interests of various nations. However, their commitment to human rights principles and universal values prevailed, and they continued to work towards a common goal. The committee held two sessions over the course of two years to finalize the text of the UDHR.

During this period, there were extensive consultations, debates, and revisions to ensure that the Declaration truly represented the fundamental rights and freedoms of all human beings. Finally, on 10 December 1948, the Universal Declaration of Human Rights was adopted by the United Nations General Assembly in Paris.

Of the 58 member states at that time, 48 voted in favor, none against, with eight abstentions and two absences.

The Declaration was proclaimed as a common standard of achievement for all peoples and all nations, affirming the inherent dignity and equal rights of every individual, regardless of nationality, race, religion, or other status. The UDHR has since become a cornerstone of international human rights law, influencing the development of numerous human rights treaties and inspiring efforts to promote and protect human rights worldwide. It's drafting process stands as a testament to the power of cooperation, dialogue, and collective action in advancing the cause of human rights for all (Vionea, 2020).

The drafting of the Universal Declaration of Human Rights (UDHR) was a collaborative and inclusive process, involving the contributions and perspectives of various delegates from different professional and ideological backgrounds. John Peters Humphrey is credited with devising the "blueprint" for the Declaration, while René Cassin composed the first draft.

The delegates from the Drafting Committee represented diverse regions and cultures, and each brought their unique perspectives to the table. Charles Malik and Cassin, influenced by the Christian Democracy movement, played a role in shaping the pro-family phrases in the Declaration. Malik, a Christian theologian, drew on different Christian sects and cited the Summa Theologica to appeal across religious lines.P.C. Chang urged for the removal of references to religion to make the document more universal and incorporated aspects of Confucianism to settle stalemates in negotiations. Hernán Santa Cruz of Chile, an educator and judge, strongly advocated for the inclusion of socioeconomic rights, which had been opposed by some Western nations.

The philosophical debate between Chang and Malik was central to the discussions, and their differing viewpoints influenced the development of the draft.

Dr. Chang emphasized the need to reflect more than just Western ideas, while Dr. Malik expounded on the philosophy of Thomas Aquinas.

Dr. Humphrey actively participated in the discussions and debates, embracing an eclectic approach to incorporate diverse perspectives.

Throughout the drafting process, the Committee considered the comments and suggestions of member states, international bodies, and various organizations. The goal was to create a comprehensive and inclusive declaration that would address the rights and freedoms of all individuals worldwide. The feedback received from different sources enriched the content of the UDHR and ensured that it reflected the concerns and aspirations of people from diverse backgrounds.

In May 1948, after approximately a year of work, the Drafting Committee held its final session, considering input from various international conferences and organizations. The hope was that an International Bill of Human Rights with legal force could be drafted and adopted alongside the Declaration. The collaborative efforts and dedication of the delegates from different regions of the world led to the creation of the Universal Declaration of Human Rights, a milestone document that set the foundation for the protection and promotion of human rights on a global scale. Its universal principles continue to inspire human rights frameworks and advocacy efforts worldwide (Hobbins, 1984).

The adoption of the Universal Declaration of Human Rights (UDHR) by the United Nations General Assembly on December 10, 1948, was a historic moment in the advancement of human rights worldwide.

Of the 58 United Nations members at the time, 48 voted in favor of the Declaration, with none against and eight abstaining. Honduras and Yemen failed to vote or abstain. Eleanor Roosevelt played a crucial role in garnering support for the Declaration's adoption, both within the United States and across the world.

Her ability to appeal to different political blocs and her dedication to promoting human rights were instrumental in the success of the Declaration.

The meeting record of the adoption provides insight into the various debates and positions taken by member states. South Africa's position was seen as an attempt to protect its apartheid system, which clearly violated several articles in the Declaration. Saudi Arabia abstained primarily due to concerns about Articles 18 and 16, related to religious freedom and equal marriage rights.

The abstentions by the communist nations were attributed to their belief that the Declaration did not sufficiently condemn fascism and national-socialism.

Eleanor Roosevelt, however, felt that the reason for the abstentions was Article 13, which provided the right of citizens to leave their countries. Others saw the Soviet bloc's opposition as a reaction to the Declaration's "negative rights," focused on civil and political rights (Jost, 2013).

While the United Kingdom voted in favor of the Declaration, its delegation expressed frustration that the document had moral obligations but lacked legal force. The absence of legal force was addressed later when the International Covenant on Civil and Political Rights came into force in 1976, giving legal status to most of the Declaration.

The 48 countries that voted in favor of the UDHR represented a diverse group of nations from various regions of the world.

Despite the central role played by the Canadian John Peters Humphrey in drafting the Declaration, the Canadian government initially abstained from voting on the draft but later voted in favor of the final version in the General Assembly.

Overall, the adoption of the Universal Declaration of Human Rights marked a significant step towards the protection and promotion of human rights globally. Over time, the Declaration has become a cornerstone of international human rights law and continues to inspire efforts to uphold the dignity and rights of all individuals worldwide. As more countries gained sovereignty and joined the United Nations later, the number of states entitled to the historical vote has increased.

The adoption of the Universal Declaration of Human Rights (UDHR) saw significant support from 48 countries, with none voting against it.

These countries were: Afghanistan, Argentina, Australia, Belgium, Bolivia, Brazil, Burma (now Myanmar), Canada, Chile, China, Colombia, Costa Rica, Cuba, Denmark, Dominican Republic, Ecuador, Egypt El Salvador, Ethiopia, France, Greece, Guatemala, Haiti, Iceland, India, Iran, Iraq, Lebanon, Liberia, Luxembourg, Mexico, Netherlands, New Zealand, Nicaragua, Norway, Pakistan, Panama, Paraguay,
Peru, Philippines, Siam (now Thailand), Sweden, Syria, Turkey, United Kingdom, United States, Uruguay, Venezuela. While the majority of countries supported the Declaration, eight countries chose to abstain from voting. These countries were:

Czechoslovakia (now split into the Czech Republic and Slovakia), Poland, Saudi Arabia

Soviet Union (now dissolved into multiple independent states), Byelorussian SSR (now Belarus), Ukrainian SSR (now Ukraine), South Africa, Yugoslavia (now dissolved into multiple independent states)

Additionally, two countries did not vote on the Declaration: Honduras, Yemen

It is important to note that at the time of voting, the number of United Nations member states was 58, and the majority of current UN member states gained sovereignty and joined the organization later, which explains the relatively small number of states entitled to the historical vote. The broad support for the Universal Declaration of Human Rights reflects the global consensus on the importance of protecting and promoting human rights for all individuals, regardless of their nationality, religion, or political affiliation.

Eleanor Roosevelt's role in promoting the UDHR as a Declaration

Eleanor Roosevelt's contributions to the drafting and promotion of the Universal Declaration of Human Rights (UDHR) were significant and far-reaching. As the first chairperson of the United Nations Commission on Human Rights, she played a central role in the formulation of the Declaration and remained committed to its principles throughout her tenure (Glendon, 2001).

Roosevelt's leadership and dedication were instrumental in guiding the Commission on Human Rights as it worked on the draft of the UDHR.

She collaborated closely with other members, including René Cassin and John Peters Humphrey, and ensured that diverse perspectives and voices were heard during the drafting process. Her ability to build consensus and bridge ideological gaps contributed to the successful crafting of a document that reflected the shared aspirations and values of humanity. In her speech in favor of the Declaration on September 28, 1948, Roosevelt eloquently described it as "the international Magna Carta of all men everywhere."

Her advocacy and passionate support helped garner widespread support for the UDHR among member states and the international community. Even after the adoption of the UDHR, Roosevelt continued to champion human rights issues within the United Nations. She served as the first United States Representative to the United Nations Commission on Human Rights and remained involved in promoting the principles of the Declaration.

Beyond her work on human rights, Roosevelt also demonstrated her commitment to addressing global issues, including hunger and malnutrition. She played a key role in supporting the creation of the Food and Agriculture Organization of the United Nations (FAO), recognizing the importance of international cooperation to tackle food security challenges.

The Food from Hunger campaign, which she helped establish, mobilized non-governmental organizations to address hunger and malnutrition worldwide. Her efforts in this area further exemplify her dedication to promoting social progress and better standards of life for all. In recognition of her outstanding contributions, the United Nations posthumously awarded Eleanor Roosevelt one of its first Human Rights Prizes in 1968. Her legacy as a tireless advocate for human rights and social justice continues to inspire and influence the global human rights movement to this day (Ruxin, 2001).

CHAPTER SIX

The UDHR's Impact on Africa

The Universal Declaration of Human Rights (UDHR), adopted by the United Nations in 1948, had a significant impact on the African continent, despite the majority of African countries still being under colonial rule at the time. The principles and values enshrined in the UDHR resonated with the aspirations of the African people and their fight for independence and self-determination.The UDHR served as an inspiration for Africa's independence movements. African leaders like Kwame Nkrumah and Patrice Lumumba invoked its principles of equality, freedom, and justice for all in their speeches, emphasizing the importance of self-determination as a basic human right.

The declaration's emphasis on equality and justice resonated with African populations facing racial discrimination and colonial oppression.

It became a rallying point for African activists and leaders seeking to dismantle systems of segregation and discrimination prevalent in colonial territories. As African countries gained independence, the UDHR influenced the shaping of their national constitutions and legal systems. The principles of human rights, democracy, and the rule of law were incorporated into the foundational documents of newly independent nations.

The UDHR's impact extended to the African Charter on Human and Peoples' Rights, adopted in 1986. This regional human rights instrument built upon the principles of the UDHR and addressed specific human rights challenges faced by the continent.

The struggle against apartheid in South Africa highlighted the tension between the principles of the UDHR and discriminatory practices of colonial powers.

Eventually, the principles of the declaration played a role in ending apartheid in 1994.

Even after Africa gained sovereignty, the UDHR remained a source of inspiration and reference for human rights advocates and activists on the continent. It continues to guide efforts to promote social justice, democracy, and respect for human dignity in contemporary Africa. In conclusion, the Universal Declaration of Human Rights played a pivotal role in shaping the discourse and fight for human rights and self-determination in Africa. Its enduring principles continue to inspire efforts to protect and promote human rights across the continent (Vijapur and Savitri, 2006).

The Universal Declaration of Human Rights (UDHR) played a crucial role in strengthening the momentum toward self-determination in Africa and inspiring liberation movements, including the fight against apartheid in South Africa.

The declaration's proclamation of universal equality, freedom, and justice resonated with the aspirations of African people seeking independence and dignity. In the post-independence era, the continent faced challenges as authoritarian and single-party regimes replaced elected governments, leading to human rights violations.

However, the principles of the UDHR continued to fuel citizens' demands for democracy and accountability.

African leaders recognized the importance of promoting human rights from an African perspective, leading to the development of the African Charter on Human and Peoples' Rights, which recognized civil, political, economic, social, and cultural rights.

In recent years, African citizens have taken to the streets to demand equality, fairness, justice, and dignity in countries like Cameroon, Kenya, Senegal, and Zimbabwe, among others.

Civil societies have become vibrant advocates for transparent and accountable governments, contributing to progress in the entrenchment of freedom of speech and association.

While challenges remain, Africa has made significant progress from its colonial past to becoming independent states with more open and pluralistic societies. The principles embodied in the UDHR continue to empower millions to advocate for progress and human rights across the continent. Humanity has moved forward, and Africa is no exception in this journey of advancement (Kuwonu, 2019).

The Universal Declaration of Human Rights (UDHR) has had a profound impact on Africa, influencing the region's understanding and promotion of human rights. Here are some of the key ways the UDHR has impacted Africa:

1. Legal Framework: The principles enshrined in the UDHR have been incorporated into many African countries' legal systems and constitutions. The UDHR has served as a model for drafting national human rights laws, ensuring that fundamental rights and freedoms are protected at the domestic level.

2. Regional Human Rights Instruments: Building on the UDHR, African nations have taken steps to address regional human rights issues. The African Charter on Human and Peoples' Rights, adopted in 1981 by the Organization of African Unity (now African Union), is one such regional instrument that reflects the principles

of the UDHR and addresses the specific human rights challenges faced by the continent.

3. Promotion of Equality and Non-Discrimination: The UDHR's commitment to equality and non-discrimination has been particularly relevant for Africa, where various ethnic, linguistic, and cultural groups coexist. The UDHR has encouraged African countries to work towards eliminating discrimination and promoting inclusivity.

4. Advancing Social and Economic Rights: The UDHR's emphasis on social and economic rights has been instrumental in shaping African countries' efforts to combat poverty, provide access to education, healthcare, and adequate living standards for their populations.

5. Empowering Civil Society: The UDHR has provided a framework for African civil society organizations to advocate for human rights, monitor government actions, and hold authorities accountable for violations.

6. Strengthening International Cooperation: The UDHR has fostered international cooperation and solidarity among African nations and the global community in addressing human rights challenges. African countries have actively participated in international forums to promote human rights and have supported efforts to address human rights issues globally.

7. Combating Colonialism and Apartheid: The UDHR's principles of self-determination and equality were crucial in the fight against colonialism and apartheid in Africa. The Declaration's influence helped garner international support for the end of colonial rule and the dismantling of apartheid in South Africa.

8. Women's Rights: The UDHR's recognition of the equal rights of men and women has contributed to advancing gender equality in Africa. The Declaration has been

instrumental in promoting women's rights and empowering women to participate in decision-making processes.

9. Human Rights Education: The UDHR has been a key tool in human rights education in Africa. It has provided a foundation for teaching and promoting human rights values in schools, universities, and community programs.

10. Inspiring Human Rights Activism: The UDHR has inspired human rights activists across Africa to advocate for justice, equality, and dignity for all. It has served as a rallying point for social movements and advocacy campaigns addressing various human rights issues on the continent.

While challenges persist, the UDHR's enduring impact on Africa demonstrates its significance as a foundational document that continues to shape the region's commitment to human rights, social justice, and peace.

Reception and adoption of the UDHR by African nations

The Universal Declaration of Human Rights (UDHR) was adopted by the United Nations General Assembly on December 10, 1948, as a common standard of achievement for all peoples and all nations. However, at that time, many African countries were still under colonial rule, and only a few were members of the United Nations. As African nations gained independence in the following decades, the UDHR played a crucial role in shaping their human rights frameworks and promoting the protection of individual rights and freedoms. Here are some key points regarding the reception and adoption of the UDHR by African nations:

1. Early Adopters: Some African countries that were already UN members at the time of the UDHR's adoption, such as Egypt, Ethiopia, Liberia, and South Africa, signed the Declaration. However, South Africa,

under its apartheid regime, did not sign the UDHR due to its discriminatory practices.

2. Inspiration for Independence Movements: The UDHR's proclamation of universal equality and human rights principles inspired many African independence movements. Leaders like Kwame Nkrumah of Ghana and Patrice Lumumba of the Democratic Republic of the Congo (DRC) emphasized the relevance of human rights, self-determination, and equality in their quest for independence.

3. African Charter on Human and Peoples' Rights: As African nations gained sovereignty and independence, they sought to develop their own regional human rights instruments. In 1981, the Organization of African Unity (now the African Union) adopted the African Charter on Human and Peoples' Rights, which is inspired by and complements the UDHR.

4. Human Rights Violations Post-Independence: In the early years of independence (the 1960s and 1970s), some African countries faced human rights challenges due to the rise of authoritarian and single-party regimes. Leaders prioritized political stability over individual rights, leading to human rights violations in some instances.

5. Progress and Advocacy: Over time, African nations have made progress in promoting human rights and democracy. Citizens across the continent have advocated for transparent and accountable governments, leading to more open and pluralistic societies. Many countries now regularly hold democratic elections and support vibrant civil societies.

6. Continued Challenges: Despite progress, challenges persist in fully realizing human rights in Africa. Issues such as poverty, conflict, corruption, and

discrimination continue to impact the enjoyment of rights and freedoms in some regions.

The UDHR's principles of freedom, equality, and justice continue to inspire African nations' efforts to advance human rights, promote democracy, and build more inclusive societies. It remains a foundational document that guides human rights protection and promotion in Africa and around the world.

Incorporation of the UDHR into domestic legal systems

The Universal Declaration of Human Rights (UDHR), as a non-binding international document, does not create legally binding obligations on its own. However, its principles and provisions have been incorporated into domestic legal systems through various mechanisms to give them legal effect and enforceability at the national level.

One common approach is constitutional incorporation, where many countries include the principles of the UDHR in their national constitutions. By doing so, these countries recognize the rights and freedoms enshrined in the UDHR as fundamental rights of their citizens, which are protected and enforceable through their domestic legal systems. Some countries have enacted specific laws or amended existing ones to reflect the principles and provisions of the UDHR. These laws address various human rights issues, such as freedom of speech, equality, non-discrimination, and protection against torture and inhumane treatment.

Courts in some countries have used the UDHR as an interpretative tool in deciding cases involving human rights issues. Judges may refer to the UDHR to give guidance on the meaning and scope of certain rights and to assess whether domestic laws or actions comply with international human rights standards.

The UDHR has also served as a foundation for subsequent human rights treaties, such as the International Covenant on Civil and Political Rights (ICCPR) and the International Covenant on Economic, Social, and Cultural Rights (ICESCR). Many countries have ratified these treaties, committing to upholding the rights and principles outlined in the UDHR at the international and domestic levels.

In some regions, like Africa, regional human rights instruments, such as the African Charter on Human and Peoples' Rights, have been developed based on the principles of the UDHR and are legally binding for the countries that have ratified them.

Additionally, governments may use the UDHR as a basis for developing public policies and practices that promote and protect human rights, even in the absence of explicit legal incorporation.

It is essential to note that the extent and manner of incorporation may vary from country to country.

Some countries may explicitly reference the UDHR in their legal texts, while others may rely more on judicial interpretation and customary practice to give effect to its principles. Ultimately, the incorporation of the UDHR into domestic legal systems reflects a country's commitment to promoting and protecting human rights within its borders.

Domestication of Law

Meaning of Domestication: While international law defines the relationship between states, it also provides for rules that states must apply within their territories. For example, international human rights law provides for obligations of states to protect the rights of persons within their jurisdiction.

To apply international law within the domestic sphere, it must be "domesticated."

This paper defines domestication as the process by which national law applies international law. A rule of international law is domesticated "when a State incorporates it and weaves it into its own domestic legislation and rule making procedures."

Domestication of a treaty or international agreement refers to the process by which the provisions of a signed and ratified treaty are integrated or adapted into the domestic law of a country. This process is essential to give the treaty the necessary legal force and effect within the national legal system, enabling its provisions to be enforceable by domestic courts. The domestication of treaties is rooted in the principle commonly found in legal systems worldwide, which holds that the status of international law or treaties in national legal systems is determined by national constitution or law, rather than by international law itself. In other words, for a treaty to have legal authority and be binding on individuals and entities within a country, it must be incorporated into the country's domestic legal framework (D'Amato, 2009).

The process of domestication can vary from one country to another, depending on its legal system and constitutional arrangements. Several methods can be employed for domesticating treaties:

1. Constitutional Incorporation: Some countries choose to incorporate the treaty's provisions directly into their constitution, making them part of the highest law of the land. This approach ensures that the treaty provisions have the highest legal standing and can be directly enforced by domestic courts.

2. Legislative Implementation: In other cases, the domestication process involves passing specific legislation that aligns with the treaty's provisions. The domestic laws are then harmonized with the treaty's requirements, ensuring that the treaty's objectives are reflected in the country's legal system.

3. Judicial Application: Domestic courts play a significant role in the domestication process by interpreting and applying treaty provisions in domestic cases. They may refer to the treaty's text, its objectives, and its relevant interpretations in international law to resolve disputes and ensure compliance with the treaty's requirements.

4. Executive Measures: The executive branch of the government may take administrative actions or issue regulations to implement the treaty's provisions. These measures can help enforce the treaty and promote its objectives within the country.

The domestication of treaties is essential to bridge the gap between international law and national legal systems. It allows countries to fulfill their treaty obligations, protect individual rights, and promote international cooperation and standards within their domestic legal framework. By incorporating treaty provisions into their domestic laws, countries ensure that international commitments are effectively enforced and upheld at the national level.

Domestication, in the context of human rights, refers to the process by which international human rights standards, such as those enshrined in the Universal Declaration of Human Rights (UDHR)

and other human rights treaties, are incorporated and made applicable in a country's domestic legal system. This process is crucial for ensuring that the rights and freedoms recognized at the international level are respected, protected, and enforceable within the country's own legal framework.

There are several methods of domesticating human rights:

1. Constitutional Incorporation: Many countries include human rights provisions, inspired by the UDHR, in their national constitutions. By doing so, these rights become fundamental and justiciable, providing citizens with legal recourse to seek remedies in domestic courts if their rights are violated.

2. Legislative Implementation: Some countries pass specific laws or amend existing legislation to align their domestic laws with international human rights standards. These laws address various human rights issues and provide detailed mechanisms for the protection and promotion of human rights.

3. Judicial Application: Courts play a critical role in domesticating human rights by interpreting and applying international human rights norms in domestic cases. Judges may rely on the UDHR and other human rights instruments to resolve disputes and assess the compatibility of domestic laws and practices with international standards.

4. Executive Actions and Policies: Governments can take executive actions and formulate policies to implement human rights principles in various areas, such as education, healthcare, and social welfare. These actions and policies are meant to align with the principles of the UDHR and promote human rights protection within the country.

5. Ratification of Human Rights Treaties: Ratifying human rights treaties, such as the ICCPR and ICESCR, signals a country's commitment to adhere to international human rights standards. Once ratified, these treaties become binding on the state, and domestic laws may need to be adjusted to comply with the treaty obligations.

6. National Human Rights Institutions: Establishing independent national human rights institutions can aid in the domestication process by monitoring human rights compliance, receiving complaints, and advocating for human rights protections.

Domestication is crucial to ensuring that international human rights standards become a reality for individuals within a country's borders. However, the degree and effectiveness of domestication may vary among countries, depending on their legal systems, political will, and commitment to human rights. Ultimately, effective domestication facilitates the promotion of human dignity, equality, and justice for all citizens.

Case studies of countries directly citing the UDHR in their municipal constitutions

Several countries have directly cited the Universal Declaration of Human Rights (UDHR) in their municipal constitutions, incorporating its principles and provisions into their national legal frameworks. Some notable case studies include:

I. India: The preamble to the Indian Constitution explicitly mentions the UDHR, and its principles have influenced various provisions in the Constitution. The Constitution of India, adopted in 1950, upholds principles of liberty, equality, and fraternity, echoing the values enshrined in the UDHR.

II. South Africa: After the end of apartheid, South Africa adopted a new constitution in 1996. The Constitution of South Africa includes a Bill of Rights that draws inspiration from the UDHR and emphasizes fundamental rights and freedoms.

III. Kenya: The Constitution of Kenya, promulgated in 2010, explicitly references the UDHR in its preamble. The Constitution protects a wide range of human rights, including civil, political, economic, social, and cultural rights, drawing on the principles of the UDHR.

IV. Nigeria: The Nigerian Constitution, particularly in its Bill of Rights, incorporates many human rights principles found in the UDHR. It has provisions that protect the right to life, liberty, and fair trial, among others.

V. Ghana: The Constitution of Ghana, adopted in 1992, references the UDHR in its preamble and includes a comprehensive Bill of Rights that safeguards various human rights and freedoms.

VI. Portugal: The Portuguese Constitution, promulgated in 1976, refers to the UDHR in its preamble. It recognizes the principles of human dignity, equality, and fundamental rights, which have their roots in the UDHR.

VII. Philippines: The 1987 Philippine Constitution acknowledges the UDHR in its preamble and includes provisions protecting individual rights and promoting social justice.

VIII. Zimbabwe: The Constitution of Zimbabwe, enacted in 2013, makes reference to the UDHR in its preamble and contains a Bill of Rights that guarantees various human rights.

These are just a few examples of countries that have incorporated the principles of the UDHR into their municipal constitutions, reflecting the global influence and significance of the Declaration on human rights protections at the national level.

UDHR in the Nigerian constitution

The Universal Declaration of Human Rights (UDHR) is an international document adopted by the United Nations in 1948.

It outlines fundamental human rights that are inherent to all individuals, regardless of their nationality, ethnicity, religion, or other characteristics. The UDHR recognizes the importance of respecting human dignity and upholding human rights to promote equality, justice, and peace worldwide.

On the other hand, the Nigerian Constitution is the supreme law of Nigeria, providing the legal framework for the governance of the country. It outlines the structure and functions of the government, the rights and responsibilities of citizens, and the legal system that governs the nation.

The connection between the UDHR and the Nigerian Constitution lies in the recognition of human rights. The Nigerian Constitution draws inspiration from the principles enshrined in the UDHR and incorporates many of its provisions to safeguard the fundamental rights of Nigerian citizens. These rights include the right to life, personal liberty, freedom of expression, and equality before the law, among others.

By incorporating the principles of the UDHR into the Nigerian Constitution, Nigeria is affirming its commitment to upholding human rights and ensuring that all individuals within its borders are entitled to these basic rights and freedoms. This alignment also demonstrates Nigeria's adherence to international human rights standards and its willingness to protect the dignity and well-being of its citizens.

The Nigerian Constitution

The Nigerian Constitution serves as the supreme law of the Federal Republic of Nigeria and provides the legal framework for the country's governance. It has undergone several revisions and amendments throughout Nigeria's history, reflecting the country's political, social, and cultural diversity (Eliagwu, 2006).

Nigeria's current constitution, enacted on May 29, 1999, marked the beginning of the Fourth Nigerian Republic.

The country's constitutional development has been influenced by its colonial past under British rule, which established the initial constitutions during the colonial era.

These early constitutions, such as the Clifford Constitution of 1922, the Richards Constitution of 1946, the Macpherson Constitution of 1951, and the Lyttleton Constitution of 1954, laid the groundwork for Nigeria's political institutions (Eyene and Garba, 2010).

Due to Nigeria's immense cultural and linguistic diversity, with over 374 multilingual groups, crafting an effective and inclusive constitution has been challenging. The country's divisions, both culturally and politically, have contributed to issues like political corruption and governance challenges. Consequently, Nigeria has experienced different forms of government, ranging from civilian to military rule, and has experimented with various systems of federalism and governance, including centrifugal and centralized federalism, presidential and parliamentary systems. The Nigerian Constitution has evolved over time to address these complexities and establish a framework for democratic governance and respect for human rights. It provides the structure of government, delineates the powers and responsibilities of different branches of government, and enshrines fundamental rights and freedoms for Nigerian citizens. As Nigeria continues to grapple with political and social challenges, the constitution remains a critical instrument for shaping the nation's future, promoting unity, and protecting the rights of its diverse population. Through periodic amendments and legal interpretations, the Nigerian Constitution seeks to adapt to the changing needs and aspirations of the country's citizens while upholding the principles of democratic governance and the rule of law (Suberu, 2019).

1999 Constitution of the Federal Republic of Nigeria
The 1999 Nigerian Constitution marked the beginning of the Fourth Nigerian Republic, establishing a federal system of democratic rule. It continues to be the supreme law of the land and is currently in force.

The constitution outlines the territorial and administrative structure of Nigeria, designating the national capital, the capitals of the 36 states, and the 774 local government areas within the country. It also establishes the three branches of government – the legislative, executive, and judicial branches – and defines their respective powers and responsibilities, as well as the separation of powers between the federal and state governments. The legislative powers are vested in the National Assembly, which consists of two chambers: the Senate and the House of Representatives. The National Assembly is responsible for making laws for the "peace, order, and good government of the Federation."

One of the significant aspects of the constitution is its recognition of fundamental human rights for every individual in Nigeria. These rights include the right to life, liberty, dignity, privacy, freedom of expression, religious freedom, and protection from slavery, violence, discrimination, and forced military service. The constitution also upholds the right to a fair and prompt trial if arrested, and the principle of presumption of innocence. Citizens also enjoy rights such as the right to own land, the right of assembly, and freedom of movement (Eliagwu, 2016).

The constitution also safeguards specific laws, such as the Land Use Act, the National Securities Agencies Act, the National Youth Service legislation, and the Public Complaints Commission Act. In 2011, President Goodluck Jonathan signed two amendments to the constitution, marking the first modifications since its enactment in 1999.

The Nigerian Constitution serves as a crucial framework for democratic governance, protecting citizens' rights and freedoms, and providing a basis for effective and equitable governance across the diverse nation of Nigeria (Shekau, 2018).

Humans Rights and the 1999 constitution of the federal republic of Nigeria

Chapter Four of the 1999 Constitution of the Federal Republic of Nigeria is titled "Fundamental Rights".

This chapter is a crucial part of the constitution as it outlines and guarantees the fundamental human rights of every Nigerian citizen. It consists of several sections that protect individual liberties and freedoms, ensuring that every citizen is treated with dignity and respect. The rights enshrined in Chapter Four are essential in promoting a just and equitable society and upholding the principles of democracy and rule of law.

The key provisions and rights contained in Chapter Four of the Nigerian Constitution include:

1. Right to Life: Section 33 guarantees the right to life, stating that no one shall be deprived of their life except in accordance with the law.

2. Right to Dignity of Human Person: Section 34 provides for the right to be treated with dignity and respect, and no one should be subjected to torture or inhuman treatment.

3. Right to Personal Liberty: Section 35 protects the right to personal liberty, ensuring that no one shall be arrested or detained except in accordance with the law.

4. Right to Fair Hearing: Section 36 guarantees the right to a fair hearing, stating that every person is entitled to a fair and public hearing within a reasonable time by an impartial court or tribunal.

5. Rights of the Accused: Section 36(5) protects the rights of the accused, including the presumption of innocence until proven guilty, the right to remain silent, and the right not to be compelled to make a confession.

6. Right to Privacy: Section 37 guarantees the right to privacy, protecting citizens' privacy, homes, correspondence, and other private affairs from unlawful interference.

7. Freedom of Thought, Conscience, and Religion: Section 38 ensures the right to freedom of thought, conscience, and religion, allowing individuals to practice and manifest their religion or belief.
8. Freedom of Expression and the Press: Section 39 protects the freedom of expression and the press, allowing individuals to express their opinions freely and access information.
9. Right to Assemble and Associate: Section 40 guarantees the right to peaceful assembly and association, allowing citizens to come together for common purposes and interests.
10. Right to Freedom of Movement: Section 41 protects the right to freedom of movement within Nigeria and the right to leave and return to the country.
11. Right to Privacy of Correspondence: Section 37(1) ensures the privacy of citizens' correspondence, including telephone conversations, telegrams, and postal communications.

These fundamental rights and liberties provided in Chapter Four of the Nigerian Constitution are crucial for upholding democracy, promoting social justice, and protecting the dignity and well-being of every Nigerian citizen. They serve as a cornerstone of the rule of law and ensure that the government respects and protects the rights of its citizens in all aspects of life.

CHAPTER SEVEN

Human Rights Challenges in Post-Colonial Africa

The process of gaining independence in Africa was marked by intense colonial liberation movements, struggles for power among the elite, and the reformation of state borders. After achieving formal sovereignty, African countries faced the challenge of establishing their own identities. However, former colonial powers continued to exert influence over their affairs, claiming to assist in state-building, economic development, and military establishment. This led to a new form of colonialism characterized by unpredictability and lack of foresight, resembling neo-patrimonialism, where legitimacy was sought, and artificial statehood created. In the postcolonial period, a new African political elite emerged, often consisting of military officials, trying to find effective paths for development while balancing tradition and modernization. Unfortunately, this process resulted in economic and political dependence on global institutions like the International Monetary Fund and the World Bank. Another significant challenge in postcolonial Africa was the blurring of borders, leading to the rise of ethno-religious problems. Attempts to address these issues often led to interventions from intra-regional non-state actors and external powers seeking to influence the resolution of conflicts. Overall, the postcolonial period in Africa has been characterized by complex challenges related to state-building, governance, economic development, and the delicate balance between tradition and modernity. These challenges have shaped Africa's political landscape and continue to influence its trajectory in the global arena (Deng, 1997).

Post-colonial Africa has faced various human rights challenges as it sought to establish and consolidate independent states.

These challenges have been shaped by historical legacies, internal conflicts, political instability, economic disparities, and social complexities. Some key human rights challenges in post-colonial Africa include:

I. Political Instability and Authoritarian Rule: Many African countries experienced prolonged periods of political instability, including military coups, civil wars, and prolonged dictatorships. Authoritarian rule often led to widespread human rights violations, including curtailment of freedom of expression, arbitrary arrests, and torture.

II. Ethnic and Tribal Tensions: Deep-rooted ethnic and tribal divisions have led to conflicts and human rights abuses in various African countries. Competition for resources, political power, and historical grievances have fueled tensions, leading to violence and discrimination against minority groups.

III. Violent Conflicts and Civil Wars: Armed conflicts have been a major human rights challenge in post-colonial Africa. Civil wars and internal armed conflicts have resulted in widespread human rights violations, including mass killings, displacement, and sexual violence.

IV. Economic Inequalities and Poverty: Many African countries face significant economic disparities and high levels of poverty. Lack of access to basic services such as education, healthcare, and clean water has been a human rights concern, particularly for vulnerable populations.

V. Corruption and Lack of Accountability: Corruption and weak governance have undermined the protection of human rights. Impunity for human rights violations by state officials has been a common issue, leading to a lack of accountability for abuses.

VI. Gender Inequality and Discrimination: Women and girls continue to face various forms of discrimination and violence in post-colonial Africa. Gender-based violence, lack of access to education and healthcare, and unequal opportunities in political and economic spheres remain significant challenges.

VII. Freedom of Expression and Media Freedom: Restrictions on freedom of expression and media freedom have been prevalent in many African countries. Journalists and activists advocating for human rights have faced harassment, intimidation, and censorship.

VIII. Refugees and Forced Displacement: Ongoing conflicts and environmental challenges have resulted in large refugee populations and internally displaced persons (IDPs). The protection and rights of refugees and IDPs have been a concern, with limited access to resources and basic services.

IX. Human Rights of Indigenous Peoples: Indigenous communities in Africa have often faced marginalization and land rights issues. Their rights to culture, language, and land have been threatened by development projects and exploitation of natural resources.

Addressing these human rights challenges requires strong institutions, respect for the rule of law, active civil society participation, and commitment from African governments and the international community to promote and protect human rights for all. Efforts towards building inclusive, accountable, and rights-based societies are essential for addressing these longstanding issues and ensuring a better future for post-colonial Africa.

Newly independent nations and the quest for human rights protection

After gaining independence, newly liberated African nations faced the crucial task of establishing and safeguarding human rights protections for their citizens.

The Universal Declaration of Human Rights (UDHR) served as a pivotal reference point in their efforts to ensure that fundamental rights and freedoms were upheld within their borders. Many of these newly independent countries integrated principles from the UDHR into their constitutions and legal frameworks, emphasizing the importance of human rights for their citizens. However, the implementation of human rights protection posed significant challenges. The quest for human rights often intersected with the complexities of nation-building, economic development, and political stability. Many African countries struggled with issues such as poverty, ethnic tensions, and weak institutions, which hindered the effective realization of human rights for all citizens. Furthermore, some governments, seeking to consolidate power, suppressed dissent and restricted civil liberties, leading to instances of human rights abuses. In some cases, these actions were justified under the pretext of maintaining stability or national security, creating tensions between human rights principles and the need for governance.

Despite these challenges, the establishment of human rights institutions and the engagement of civil society played essential roles in advocating for human rights and holding governments accountable.

Human rights organizations, activists, and the media became critical forces in pushing for greater respect for human rights and demanding accountability from governments.

Over time, African countries have made progress in advancing human rights protections. Regional human rights mechanisms, such as the African Charter on Human and Peoples' Rights and the African Court on Human and Peoples' Rights, have been established to strengthen the promotion and protection of human rights across the continent.

However, the quest for human rights protection remains an ongoing journey.

Many African nations still grapple with challenges related to political instability, corruption, and inequality, which continue to impact the full realization of human rights for all citizens. Nonetheless, the commitment to upholding human rights and promoting accountability remains central to the region's aspirations for a more just and equitable future.

Addressing systemic issues of discrimination and inequality

Addressing systemic issues of discrimination and inequality is essential for promoting human rights and building more inclusive and just societies in Africa. These issues are deeply rooted in historical, social, economic, and political structures, and tackling them requires comprehensive and sustained efforts at various levels.

1. Legal Reforms: African countries can start by reviewing and reforming their legal frameworks to eliminate discriminatory laws and ensure that all citizens are equal before the law. This includes revising constitutions, penal codes, and other legislation to prohibit discrimination based on race, ethnicity, gender, religion, disability, or any other grounds.

2. Human Rights Education: Promoting human rights education is crucial for fostering a culture of respect and understanding among individuals and communities. Schools, universities, and civil society organizations can play a significant role in educating people about their rights and the importance of respecting the rights of others.

3. Empowerment of Marginalized Groups: Empowering marginalized groups, such as women, ethnic minorities, persons with disabilities, and LGBTQ+ individuals, is vital for breaking the cycle of discrimination and inequality. This can be achieved through targeted policies and programs that provide equal access to education, healthcare, employment opportunities, and political participation.

4. Strengthening Institutions: Building strong and independent institutions, including the judiciary and human rights commissions, is crucial for ensuring that human rights violations are addressed and justice is served. Institutions must have the capacity to investigate and address complaints of discrimination and inequality.

5. Public Awareness Campaigns: Governments and civil society can engage in public awareness campaigns to raise awareness about the harmful effects of discrimination and inequality. These campaigns can challenge stereotypes and promote a more inclusive and tolerant society.

6. Economic Empowerment: Addressing economic disparities is essential for combating inequality. Governments can implement policies that promote inclusive economic growth, provide social safety nets, and ensure equitable access to resources and opportunities.

7. Addressing Intersectionality: Recognizing that individuals may face multiple forms of discrimination due to the intersection of various identities (e.g., gender, race, and disability) is crucial. Policies and programs should be designed to address these intersecting forms of discrimination.

8. Accountability and Transparency: Governments must be accountable for their actions and policies related to discrimination and inequality. This includes reporting on progress and challenges in promoting human rights, as well as providing avenues for citizens to hold authorities accountable.

9. Regional and International Cooperation: Collaboration between African countries and regional and international organizations can support efforts to address systemic issues of discrimination and

inequality. Regional human rights mechanisms and peer learning can facilitate best practices and support countries in their human rights endeavors.

10. Inclusive Governance: Inclusive governance that involves all segments of society in decision-making processes is essential for addressing systemic issues. Governments should actively engage civil society, marginalized groups, and other stakeholders in policy development and implementation.

Addressing systemic issues of discrimination and inequality requires sustained commitment, collective action, and a multi-dimensional approach that addresses the root causes and promotes a culture of human rights and inclusivity.

Human rights abuses under authoritarian regimes in Africa

The end of colonial rule in Africa brought forth newly independent states facing the challenges of state-building and nation-building. Initially adopting democratic constitutions from their former colonizers, many African countries soon descended into various forms of authoritarianism.

This shift towards authoritarian rule during the Cold War was influenced by various factors, including the legacy of colonial authoritarianism, the ideological battles of the era, the military's organizational advantages, ethno-political competition, and traditional political culture.

However, the "Third Wave of Democratization" in the 1990s ushered in a new era of constitutionalism, rule of law, multiparty elections, and power alternance. Democracy became the norm in Africa, although flawed, with many governments coming to power through competitive elections and civilian leadership prevailing over military rule.

Despite this progress, challenges to democracy persist. Some rulers have established family dynasties or ethnic clan-based neo-patrimonial systems of rule. New military rulers have emerged through coups or in failed states.

Additionally, parties and presidents have learned to manipulate elections to stay in power, denying basic freedoms and engaging in fraudulent practices. Post-election violence has also become a concern, reflecting discontent and serving as a campaign technique. Researchers have focused on conflict resolution and electoral studies to understand this phenomenon and its impact on democracy building. The development of civil society and social movements has also been emphasized as essential for democracy (Yates, 2021).

Critiques of Western-style democracy for Africa and discussions on alternative forms of government based on indigenous cultural experience highlight the diversity of democratic practices. While some African countries are experiencing democratic decline, others are consolidating their democracies, showing that the suitability of democracy to African conditions depends on the quality of leadership, political institutions, and external support.

In conclusion, Africa's journey towards democracy has been marked by progress, challenges, and complexities. While many countries have made strides in consolidating democratic governance, others continue to grapple with authoritarian tendencies and political manipulation. The future of democracy in Africa will depend on the collective efforts of leaders, institutions, civil society, and the international community to promote inclusive, accountable, and participatory governance.

CHAPTER EIGHT

Struggles for Justice and Accountability in Africa

Struggles for justice and accountability in Africa have been significant and multifaceted, reflecting the continent's complex history of colonialism, post-colonial governance, and challenges related to human rights and the rule of law. One prominent approach to addressing past human rights abuses and atrocities in some African countries is the establishment of Truth and Reconciliation Commissions (TRCs). These commissions aim to investigate and address historical injustices, promote reconciliation, and provide a platform for victims to share their experiences. Examples include South Africa's TRC, which played a crucial role in post-apartheid healing, and Sierra Leone's TRC, which dealt with the legacy of its civil war.

The International Criminal Court (ICC) has also been involved in prosecuting individuals responsible for war crimes, crimes against humanity, and genocide in Africa. Some leaders, such as Sudanese President Omar al-Bashir and former Liberian President Charles Taylor, have faced ICC indictments for their alleged roles in atrocities.

African civil society organizations play a vital role in advocating for justice, human rights, and accountability. They mobilize public support, document abuses, and demand accountability from both state and non-state actors. Anti-corruption efforts are ongoing in many African countries, as corruption remains a significant challenge that undermines justice and accountability.

Some countries have established anti-corruption agencies, and civil society groups are actively involved in monitoring and exposing corrupt practices. Transitional justice initiatives are adopted by many African countries, combining legal and non-legal approaches to address past human rights violations.

These initiatives include reparations for victims, memorialization projects, and institutional reforms to prevent future abuses. Land and resource rights often lead to conflicts and human rights violations in Africa. Activists and communities work to assert their rights and demand fair and equitable access to resources.

Women's rights activists in Africa are working to address gender-based violence, discrimination, and unequal access to justice. Efforts include legal reforms, awareness campaigns, and support for victims of gender-based violence. Journalists and media organizations face challenges in many African countries, with restrictions on press freedom and harassment of reporters. Advocates work to protect media freedom and ensure journalists can report without fear of reprisals.

Many marginalized communities in Africa, such as indigenous peoples and minorities, face barriers to accessing justice. Efforts are underway to address these inequalities and promote inclusive justice systems. The struggles for justice and accountability in Africa continue to evolve, with ongoing challenges and opportunities for positive change. Civil society, human rights organizations, international institutions, and concerned individuals all play crucial roles in advancing these causes and promoting a more just and accountable continent.

The fight against apartheid in South Africa

The fight against apartheid in South Africa was a historic and prolonged struggle for justice, equality, and human rights. Apartheid was a system of institutionalized racial segregation and discrimination enforced by the government of South Africa between 1948 and the early 1990s. It aimed to maintain white minority rule and suppress the rights and freedoms of the majority Black population.

The African National Congress (ANC) played a central role in leading the anti-apartheid movement. Established in 1912, the ANC initially pursued peaceful protests and petitions against discriminatory laws.

However, as the apartheid regime became more oppressive, the ANC and other resistance groups shifted towards more assertive and direct actions.One significant turning point in the struggle against apartheid was the Sharpeville Massacre in 1960. On March 21, police opened fire on a peaceful protest against pass laws, killing 69 people and injuring hundreds. This event garnered international attention and condemnation, leading to increased support for the anti-apartheid movement and putting pressure on the South African government. In response to the growing resistance, the apartheid government intensified its repression and imposed harsh measures to suppress dissent. The ANC and other anti-apartheid organizations, including the Pan Africanist Congress (PAC), were banned, and their leaders were arrested and imprisoned.

The armed struggle gained momentum in the 1960s and 1970s, with the establishment of the ANC's military wing, Umkhonto we Sizwe (MK), led by figures such as Nelson Mandela and Oliver Tambo.

MK engaged in acts of sabotage against government infrastructure and strategic targets to disrupt the apartheid regime. International solidarity played a crucial role in the fight against apartheid.

The United Nations, various countries, and international organizations imposed economic and cultural sanctions on South Africa, isolating the country and pressuring the government to end apartheid policies. The Soweto Uprising in 1976 marked another significant moment in the struggle. Students in Soweto protested against the compulsory use of Afrikaans as the language of instruction, leading to violent clashes with the police.

The Soweto Uprising further galvanized opposition to apartheid both domestically and globally.

As resistance grew, the apartheid regime faced mounting internal and external pressure to dismantle the discriminatory system.

In 1990, President F.W. de Klerk announced the end of apartheid and the unbanning of the ANC, PAC, and other anti-apartheid organizations. Negotiations between the ANC and the apartheid government followed, leading to the release of Nelson Mandela from prison in 1990 after 27 years of incarceration. In 1994, South Africa held its first democratic and inclusive elections, with Mandela elected as the country's first Black president. This marked the official end of apartheid and the beginning of a new era of democracy and equality in South Africa. The fight against apartheid in South Africa stands as a powerful example of the resilience and determination of a people to overcome injustice and oppression. It remains a symbol of the transformative power of collective action, international solidarity, and the pursuit of human rights and social justice.

MK (Mkhonto We Sizwe) soldiers toyi-toyi at
Chris Hani's funeral, Soweto, 1993

Background to Apartheid

The fight against apartheid in South Africa was a long and arduous struggle against racial segregation and discrimination. Apartheid, an Afrikaans word meaning "separateness," was a system enforced by the South African government, aiming to maintain white minority rule and suppress the rights and freedoms of the Black population. The roots of racial discrimination in South Africa can be traced back to the early days of European colonization in the 17th century. Large-scale colonization by the Dutch East India Company displaced the local Khoikhoi people, replaced them with white settlers, and brought in Black slaves from across the Dutch Empire. Slaves required passes to travel away from their masters, and pass laws were later extended to the Khoikhoi and other Africans, further restricting their movement.

In the 19th century, legislation was passed to limit the freedom of unskilled workers and regulate race relations. The discovery of diamonds and gold exacerbated racial inequality between whites and blacks. Various laws were enacted to disenfranchise non-white voters, segregate communities, and restrict land ownership for non-whites. The 20th century saw the formal establishment of apartheid as a state policy. Acts such as the Franchise and Ballot Act of 1892 and the Glen Grey Act of 1894 deprived non-white voters of their rights. Pass laws were further enforced, and segregationist policies were implemented under the South African Native Affairs Commission (Gish, 2004).

The Union of South Africa, established in 1910, continued the legislative program of racial segregation, giving complete political control to white people while removing the right of black people to sit in parliament. Various acts, such as the Native Land Act of 1913 and the Urban Areas Act of 1923, enforced residential segregation and provided cheap labor for white-led industries (Tankard, 2004).

World War II brought some relaxation in the enforcement of segregationist laws, but growing opposition from Afrikaner nationalists led to the strengthening of apartheid policies after the war. The 1948 South African general election saw the victory of the Herenigde Nasionale Party, which embraced strict apartheid policies. The struggle against apartheid intensified with the formation of the African National Congress (ANC) and other resistance groups. Mass protests, international sanctions, and the armed struggle led by the ANC's military wing, Umkhonto we Sizwe, put immense pressure on the apartheid regime.

In 1990, President F.W. de Klerk announced the end of apartheid and the unbanning of anti-apartheid organizations, including the ANC. Negotiations between the ANC and the apartheid government followed, leading to the release of Nelson Mandela from prison in 1990. In 1994, South Africa held its first democratic and inclusive elections, with Mandela elected as the country's first Black president. This marked the official end of apartheid and the beginning of a new era of democracy and equality in South Africa. The fight against apartheid in South Africa stands as a testament to the power of collective action, international solidarity, and the unwavering pursuit of justice and human rights. It serves as a crucial reminder of the importance of standing against all forms of discrimination and oppression (Clark and William, 2023).

Headshot of the last president of Apartheid South Africa: F.W. de Klerk

By Rachel Hatch February 10, 2019

Institutionalization of Apartheid

The fight against apartheid in South Africa was a significant struggle against racial segregation and discrimination. Apartheid, meaning "separateness," was a system enforced by the South African government to maintain white minority rule and suppress the rights of the Black population. The roots of racial discrimination in South Africa can be traced back to European colonization in the 17th century, which displaced indigenous people and introduced slavery. Over time, various laws were passed to limit the rights and opportunities of non-white populations, leading to significant gaps in social structure and discontent among urban Black communities.

The post-World War II economic boom attracted black migrant workers to industrial centers, exacerbating overcrowding and social issues due to the government's failure to accommodate the influx with proper housing and services.

In response, black political organizations like the African National Congress (ANC) and others emerged, demanding political rights, land reform, and the right to unionize. As the government's efforts to curtail the evolving position of nonwhites proved ineffective, the Herenigde Nasionale Party (National Party) capitalized on the discontent and offered a policy of apartheid as a means of preserving white domination. Apartheid was the systematic segregation of races through parliamentary acts and administrative decrees, aiming to remove blacks from areas designated for whites (Kaplan, 2015).

The National Party's adoption of apartheid as its ideological foundation and practical policy led to its victory in the 1948 South African general election. Under the leadership of Prime Minister Daniel François Malan, apartheid was implemented, silencing liberal opposition and promoting white supremacy. The implementation of apartheid was not without factional differences within the National Party. Some favored systematic segregation with controlled black labor to advance economic gains for Afrikaners, while others believed in complete separation of races, with blacks living in native reserves and having separate political and economic structures (Meredith, 2015).

Despite the factional differences, apartheid became the prevailing policy in South Africa, leading to widespread oppression and discrimination against non-white populations. The fight against apartheid continued for decades, with mass protests, international sanctions, and the leadership of figures like Nelson Mandela and the ANC playing crucial roles. In 1990, President F.W. de Klerk announced the end of apartheid, and negotiations between the ANC and the apartheid government led to the dismantling of the system.

In 1994, South Africa held its first democratic elections, with Nelson Mandela becoming the country's first Black president, symbolizing the official end of apartheid and the beginning of a new era of democracy and equality in the nation (Cole, 2010).

Apartheid Legislation

The apartheid regime in South Africa was characterized by a systematic and institutionalized separation of racial groups, enforced through a series of discriminatory laws. The National Party, which came to power in 1948, argued that South Africa comprised four distinct racial groups: white, black, Coloured, and Indian, and it divided these groups into 13 nations or racial federations. The regime passed laws that constituted "grand apartheid," aimed at large-scale racial segregation by compelling people to live in separate areas defined by their race. This approach was influenced by the British rule, which also practiced racial separation after the Anglo-Boer War (Ungar, 1989).

Key apartheid laws included the Population Registration Act of 1950, which formalized racial classification and required identity cards specifying racial groups for individuals over 18. The Group Areas Act of 1950 designated separate living areas based on race, leading to forced removals of non-whites from diverse neighborhoods. Other laws like the Prevention of Illegal Squatting Act of 1951 demolished black shanty towns and required white employers to provide housing for black workers. The Native Laws Amendment Act of 1952 centralized and tightened pass laws, restricting black people's stay in urban areas without permits. Marriage and sexual relations between different races were criminalized under the Prohibition of Mixed Marriages Act of 1949 and the Immorality Act of 1950. The Reservation of Separate Amenities Act of 1953 segregated public facilities like beaches, buses, hospitals, schools, and universities (Beck, 2000).

The Suppression of Communism Act of 1950 banned the Communist Party and any opposition to government policies, suppressing resistance to apartheid.

Various acts, including the Bantu Education Act of 1953 and the Promotion of Black Self-Government Act of 1959, established separate structures and education systems for blacks, promoting the policy of separate development in the bantustans. The regime tightened pass laws, required blacks to carry identity documents, and restricted their movement, especially women's, to prevent immigration and enforce racial segregation. Apartheid policies provoked widespread resistance, leading to mass arrests, bannings, and trials of opposition leaders. The struggle against apartheid continued until 1990 when the apartheid system was dismantled, and South Africa transitioned to a democratic and inclusive society under the leadership of Nelson Mandela and the ANC (Clark, and Worger, 2016).

Disenfranchisement of Coloured voters

In 1950, under the leadership of D. F. Malan, the National Party (NP) announced its intention to establish a Coloured Affairs Department. Following Malan's tenure, J.G. Strijdom, the succeeding Prime Minister, pursued further discriminatory measures against black and Coloured residents of the Cape Province. In 1951, the Separate Representation of Voters Bill was introduced, seeking to strip voting rights from black and Coloured residents of the Cape Province. However, the bill was challenged in court by four voters with support from the United Party. The Cape Supreme Court initially upheld the act, but it was later declared invalid by the Appeal Court, which ruled that a two-thirds majority in a joint sitting of both Houses of Parliament was required to change the entrenched clauses of the Constitution. In response, the government introduced the High Court of Parliament Bill in 1952, attempting to give Parliament the power to overrule court decisions. However, the Cape Supreme Court and the Appeal Court declared this bill invalid as well (Muller, 1975). .

In 1955, the Strijdom government increased the number of judges in the Appeal Court and appointed pro-Nationalist judges to fill the new positions.

Additionally, the government introduced the Senate Act, which expanded the Senate and heavily favored NP control, allowing them to pass the Separate Representation of Voters Act in 1956. This act transferred Coloured voters from the common voters' roll to a separate Coloured voters' roll. After passing this act, the Senate was restored to its original size. The Senate Act was contested in the Supreme Court, but the recently expanded Appeal Court, filled with government-supporting judges, upheld the act along with the Act to remove Coloured voters. Initially, the 1956 law allowed Coloureds to elect four representatives to Parliament. However, a subsequent law in 1969 abolished those seats and stripped Coloureds of their right to vote, leaving only whites as the sole enfranchised group, as Indians had never been granted the right to vote. These discriminatory laws were part of the apartheid regime's efforts to suppress the political rights of non-white citizens in South Africa (Du Pre, 1994).

Bantustan (Homeland System)

The apartheid government in South Africa implemented the homeland system, also known as Bantustan policy, with the aim of dividing the country into separate states, each intended to become a nation-state for different ethnic groups. This policy was part of the broader strategy of "separate development" and was initiated when Hendrik Verwoerd became Prime Minister in 1958. Under this system, the government designated certain areas as homelands and reserved 13 percent of the land for black South Africans, mostly in economically unproductive regions. The Tomlinson Commission of 1954 supported apartheid and the homeland system, suggesting that more land should be given to the homelands, but this recommendation was not fully implemented (Evans, 1997).

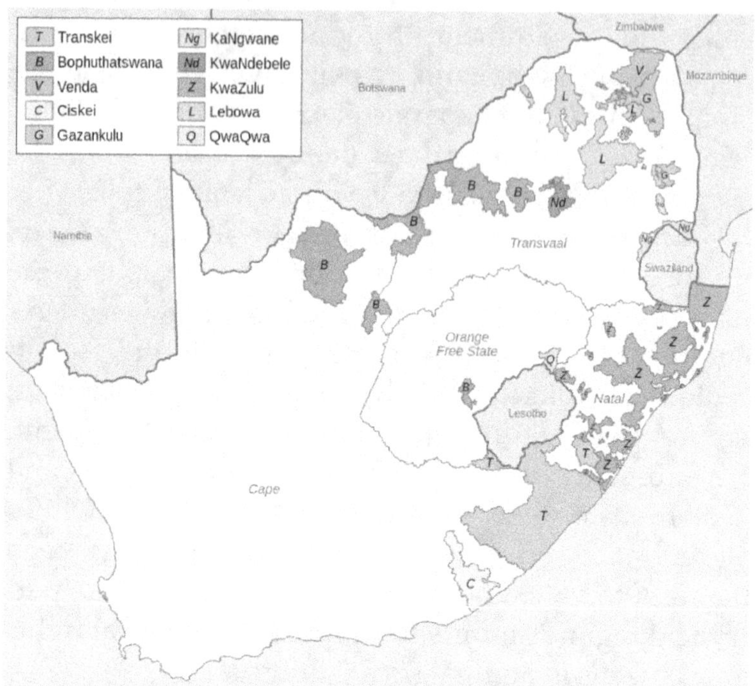

Map of the black homelands in South Africa at the end of apartheid in 1994

CC BY-SA 3, File:Bantustans in South Africa.svg | Created: 8 May 2013

The idea behind the homeland system was to grant independence to these designated areas, making their inhabitants citizens of the independent homelands rather than citizens of South Africa. The government justified this policy by claiming it was not about racial discrimination but about recognizing different nations and granting them self-determination within their respective homelands.

In practice, the homelands were economically underdeveloped and geographically fragmented, leading to significant challenges for their inhabitants. Black South Africans were forcibly removed from cities to live in these homelands, even if they had no historical or cultural ties to the designated areas.

The government established border industries and the Bantu Investment Corporation to promote economic development in or near the homelands (Evans, 1997).

In total, 20 homelands were allocated, 19 for black ethnic groups, and one, Basterland, for a sub-group of Coloureds known as Basters. Four of the homelands were declared independent by the South African government: Transkei, Bophuthatswana, Venda, and Ciskei (known as the TBVC states). Once a homeland gained nominal independence, its designated citizens lost their South African citizenship and became citizens of their homeland. The homeland policy was widely criticized both domestically and internationally for perpetuating racial segregation and marginalizing black South Africans. The system eventually collapsed with the end of apartheid in the early 1990s, and the homelands were reincorporated into a unified South Africa (Amisi and Simphiwe, 2008).

Khayelitsha township in Cape Town, where blacks were sent during the apartheid policy of segregation

Source: Folha de S.paulo

International Recognition of the Bantustan

The Bantustan system in South Africa and South West Africa (now Namibia) was classified into three categories based on their degree of nominal self-rule: "non-self-governing", "self-governing", and "independent." The South African government aimed to create separate states for different ethnic groups, but in reality, the Bantustans were little more than puppet states controlled by South Africa. The self-governing Bantustans had some level of control over their internal affairs, but they were not fully sovereign nations. The independent Bantustans, including Transkei, Bophutatswana, Venda, and Ciskei (also known as the TBVC states), were intended to be fully sovereign, but they lacked significant economic infrastructure and were geographically fragmented. Despite their lack of genuine sovereignty, South Africa remained the only country to recognize the independence of these Bantustans. However, internal organizations of many countries, as well as the South African government, lobbied for their recognition. For instance, the Swiss-South African Association encouraged the Swiss government to recognize Transkei when it was founded. In 1976, as the United States House of Representatives considered a resolution urging the President not to recognize Transkei, the South African government actively lobbied lawmakers to oppose the bill.

Each TBVC state extended recognition to the other independent Bantustans, and South Africa showed its commitment to the notion of TBVC sovereignty by establishing embassies in the TBVC capitals. Despite these efforts, the international community largely regarded the Bantustans as part of South Africa's apartheid policy and did not recognize their independence as genuine sovereign states. Ultimately, the Bantustan system was dismantled with the end of apartheid in the early 1990s, and all regions were reintegrated into a unified South Africa (Pitterman, 1978).

Rise of ANC and Mkhonto we Sizwe (MK)

The rise of the African National Congress (ANC) and its armed wing, Umkhonto we Sizwe (MK), was a pivotal development in the struggle against apartheid in South Africa. The ANC, founded in 1912, initially pursued peaceful means to fight racial discrimination and advocate for the rights of black South Africans. However, faced with brutal government repression and the inadequacy of nonviolent strategies, the ANC established MK in 1961 as an armed resistance movement. Under the leadership of Nelson Mandela and other ANC leaders, MK conducted acts of sabotage against apartheid institutions and symbols, aiming to draw international attention to the injustices and force the government to negotiate. MK's actions, along with the broader anti-apartheid movement, garnered significant global support and led to economic sanctions on South Africa, isolating the apartheid regime. This, combined with internal protests and negotiations, ultimately brought about the end of apartheid. In 1994, South Africa held its first democratic elections, with the ANC winning and Mandela becoming the country's first black president. The rise of the ANC and MK represents the determination of the South African people to fight for justice, equality, and human rights, leaving a lasting impact on the nation's history and inspiring movements for freedom worldwide.

Nelson Mandela during the treason trial. Johannesburg 1958. Source: oxy.edu

Role of Nelson Mandela

Nelson Mandela played a central and transformative role in the struggle against apartheid and the subsequent establishment of a democratic and inclusive South Africa. His contributions can be summarized in several key aspects:

1. Leadership in the ANC: Mandela joined the African National Congress (ANC) in the 1940s and became an influential member of the party's leadership. He helped to shape the ANC's strategy and vision for a non-racial and democratic South Africa.

2. Nonviolent Resistance: In the early years of his activism, Mandela advocated for nonviolent resistance against apartheid. He participated in peaceful protests and advocated for equal rights and justice for all South Africans.

3. MK and Armed Struggle: As apartheid repression intensified and peaceful means proved inadequate, Mandela co-founded Umkhonto we Sizwe (MK), the armed wing of the ANC. MK conducted acts of sabotage against government institutions and infrastructure, aiming to draw international attention to the injustices of apartheid.

4. Imprisonment and Symbolic Resistance: In 1962, Mandela was arrested and sentenced to life in prison for his anti-apartheid activities. During his 27 years of imprisonment, he became a symbol of resistance and resilience, inspiring both South Africans and the international community to continue the fight against apartheid.

5. Negotiations and Reconciliation: In the late 1980s and early 1990s, as international pressure and internal resistance mounted, the apartheid government initiated negotiations with Mandela and other ANC leaders. Mandela played a key role in these negotiations,

leading to the peaceful transition to democracy and the end of apartheid.

6. Transition to Democracy: After his release from prison in 1990, Mandela led the ANC in negotiations with the government, culminating in the historic 1994 elections. Mandela's leadership and commitment to reconciliation helped to ease tensions and unite South Africans during this critical period.

7. First Black President: In 1994, Mandela was elected as the first black President of South Africa. His presidency was characterized by efforts to heal the wounds of apartheid, promote racial reconciliation, and build a new, inclusive South Africa.

8. Humanitarian Legacy: Mandela's commitment to human rights and social justice extended beyond South Africa's borders. He was an advocate for peace and played a significant role in various global humanitarian causes.

Nelson Mandela's leadership, courage, and commitment to justice made him a global symbol of the struggle against oppression and discrimination. His legacy continues to inspire people worldwide to work towards a more just and equitable world.

Role of Outside Forces

The fight against apartheid in South Africa was not only a domestic struggle but also garnered significant international support. Several countries, governments, and international organizations played vital roles in putting pressure on the apartheid regime and contributing to its eventual dismantling. Here are some key roles played by other countries in the fight against apartheid.

1. Economic Sanctions: Many countries imposed economic sanctions on South Africa to isolate the apartheid regime economically. These sanctions targeted trade, investment, and financial transactions,

aiming to put economic pressure on the government to change its discriminatory policies.

2. Diplomatic Isolation: The international community, through various diplomatic efforts, sought to isolate the apartheid government and withdraw recognition of its legitimacy. Diplomatic efforts included condemning apartheid in international forums, expelling South African ambassadors, and refusing to participate in sports and cultural events hosted by South Africa.

3. Boycotts and Divestment: Grassroots movements and international organizations led boycott and divestment campaigns to encourage businesses, universities, and institutions to divest from South Africa and disengage from supporting the apartheid regime financially.

4. United Nations: The United Nations played a significant role in condemning apartheid and supporting the anti-apartheid movement. In 1962, the UN passed a resolution calling for sanctions against South Africa, and in 1973, it recognized the ANC as the legitimate representative of the South African people.

5. Armed Struggle Support: Several countries, particularly those sympathetic to the anti-apartheid cause, provided support to the African National Congress (ANC) and its armed wing, Umkhonto we Sizwe (MK). This assistance included military training, funding, and safe havens for ANC activists.

6. Sporting and Cultural Boycotts: Sports and cultural boycotts were effective tools in raising awareness about apartheid and putting pressure on South Africa's government. Many international sports bodies, artists, and musicians refused to participate in events in South Africa.

7. Support for Exiled Leaders: Countries like Zambia and Tanzania provided sanctuary and support for exiled anti-apartheid leaders, including Nelson Mandela and

other ANC members, allowing them to continue their struggle from abroad.

8. Academic and Cultural Exchange: Academic institutions and cultural organizations in various countries refused to collaborate with South African universities and cultural institutions that upheld apartheid policies.

9. Anti-Apartheid Movements: Civil society movements in different countries, including student groups, churches, labor unions, and human rights organizations, organized protests, marches, and campaigns to raise awareness about apartheid and mobilize support for its end.

The collective efforts of these countries and international organizations contributed significantly to the eventual demise of apartheid in South Africa and the establishment of a democratic and non-racial society. The fight against apartheid remains a powerful example of the impact of global solidarity in promoting human rights and social justice.

Human rights abuses during Apartheid

During the apartheid era in South Africa, which lasted from 1948 to the early 1990s, the government implemented a system of institutionalized racial segregation and discrimination that led to severe human rights abuses against the majority black population. Some of the key human rights abuses during apartheid include:

1. Racial Discrimination: Apartheid laws enforced strict racial segregation, categorizing people into racial groups and restricting their movement and access to public services based on their race. This systemic discrimination violated the principles of equality and non-discrimination.

2. Forced Removals: The government forcibly removed millions of black South Africans from their homes and relocated them to designated areas known as

"homelands" or "townships." These forced removals resulted in the destruction of vibrant communities and caused immense suffering to those displaced.

3. Pass Laws: The Pass Laws required black people to carry identification documents (passes) at all times, restricting their movement and employment opportunities. Violations of the pass laws often led to arrests, detention, and brutal punishment.

4. Separate Amenities Act: Black South Africans were denied access to the same facilities and services as white citizens. Public amenities, such as schools, hospitals, and parks, were racially segregated, with separate and unequal facilities for different racial groups.

5. Bantu Education: The government introduced a separate and inferior education system for black South Africans known as Bantu Education. The curriculum was designed to perpetuate racial stereotypes and limit opportunities for black students.

6. Police Brutality and Torture: Security forces often used excessive force and torture against black activists and political opponents. Black detainees were subjected to cruel treatment and inhumane conditions in prisons.

7. Restrictions on Freedom of Expression: The government imposed strict censorship on the media and restricted freedom of speech to control information and suppress dissenting voices.

8. Systematic Repression of Opposition: Anti-apartheid activists, including members of the African National Congress (ANC) and other political organizations, were harassed, arrested, and imprisoned. Many were subject to banning orders, which restricted their movement and communication.

9. Massacre and Violence: The government responded violently to anti-apartheid protests, leading to

numerous massacres, such as the Sharpeville Massacre in 1960 and the Soweto Uprising in 1976, resulting in the deaths of unarmed protesters.

Denial of Citizenship and Political Rights: Black South Africans were denied citizenship and the right to participate in the national government, leaving them disenfranchised and without a voice in the country's governance. These human rights abuses sparked international condemnation and calls for the dismantling of the apartheid system. The global anti-apartheid movement, combined with internal resistance and international pressure, eventually led to the end of apartheid and the establishment of a democratic South Africa in the early 1990s, with Nelson Mandela becoming the country's first black president in 1994.

Nigeria's civil rights movements and challenges to democracy

May 29, 1999, was a significant moment in Nigeria's history as it marked the beginning of the fourth Republic, signaling the end of military misrule marked by suffering, decayed infrastructure, and widespread corruption. The return to democratic rule brought hope for a just and equal society, and Nigerians welcomed it with optimism, expecting stability, peace, and prosperity. However, twelve years later, Nigerians still await the fulfillment of "democracy dividends," such as social welfare, justice, equity, and equal access to resources and power

Several critical governance problems continue to challenge democratic governance in Nigeria.

These include leadership challenges, corruption, lack of transparency, the need for constitutional and electoral reforms, rising civil strife, poverty, unemployment, godfatherism, and issues related to human security and human rights.

Although all these challenges are crucial, in this write-up, we focus on five immediate and recurring pitfalls:

Leadership challenges, Corruption, Human rights, Civil strife, and Electoral reforms. Throughout Nigeria's history, civil rights movements have been instrumental in advocating for human rights, social justice, and political representation. These movements originated from the anti-colonial struggle against British rule, seeking independence and self-determination.

They also fought against slavery and oppressive colonial practices even before Nigeria gained independence. The Nigerian women's movement played a significant role, advocating for gender equality, women's rights, and political representation.

Additionally, the pro-democracy movement emerged during periods of military rule, pushing for a return to civilian rule and democratic governance. However, Nigeria has faced challenges to its democracy. Frequent military interventions resulted in prolonged military rule, posing threats to democratic governance and political stability. The country's diversity in terms of ethnic groups and religious affiliations also led to ethnic and religious tensions, challenging national unity and inclusivity.

Electoral irregularities, voter fraud, and political manipulation have affected the credibility and legitimacy of Nigeria's electoral processes. Human rights concerns, including police brutality and extrajudicial killings, have been raised by civil rights movements advocating for reforms. Inequality and poverty have been persistent challenges, with civil rights movements fighting for social and economic justice and equitable development. Secessionist movements in different regions, like the Biafra movement in the southeast, have posed challenges to national unity and stability. Despite these obstacles, civil rights movements in Nigeria continue to advocate for democratic reforms and human rights protection. The country has made progress in transitioning to civilian rule and strengthening democratic institutions, but further efforts are needed to address the remaining challenges and build a more inclusive and resilient democracy (Adeniji, 2003).

Governance in Nigeria, particularly good governance, has been a significant challenge. Good governance encompasses participatory, transparent, accountable, effective, equitable, and consensus-oriented practices that promote the rule of law and prioritize the needs of the citizens, especially the poorest and most vulnerable.

1. Leadership Challenges: Nigeria has struggled with the quality of its leadership. Many leaders have prioritized self-enrichment over the welfare of the citizens. Lack of visionary and transformative leaders has hindered progress and development.

2. Corruption: Corruption has been pervasive in Nigeria, affecting various sectors and eroding public trust. Political leaders and institutions have been involved in embezzlement and bribery, hindering effective governance and service delivery.

3. Human Rights: Despite improvements, human rights violations persist. Extrajudicial killings, arbitrary arrests, and poor prison conditions have been reported.

The protection and enjoyment of fundamental rights are undermined by weak infrastructure and socio-economic challenges.

4. Civil Strife: Nigeria's diversity and history of military rule have contributed to civil strife and conflicts. Political, ethnic, and religious tensions have led to recurrent skirmishes, further complicating governance and stability.

5. Electoral Reforms: Nigeria's electoral process has faced challenges with irregularities and allegations of vote manipulation. Free and fair elections are essential for democratic governance, and controversies surrounding elections can undermine the legitimacy of the government.

Addressing these challenges requires comprehensive reforms and efforts from both government and civil society.

Building strong institutions, enhancing transparency, fighting corruption, safeguarding human rights, promoting inclusivity, and ensuring meaningful electoral reforms are crucial steps toward achieving good democratic governance in Nigeria. (Olu-Adeyemi, 2004).

Seeking justice for genocide in Rwanda The Rwandan genocide occurred between April 7 and July 15, 1994, during the Rwandan Civil War. It resulted in the targeted killings of members of the Tutsi minority ethnic group, as well as some moderate Hutu and Twa individuals, by armed Hutu militias. The death toll is estimated to be between 500,000 to 662,000 Tutsi deaths.The genocide was preceded by the Rwandan Civil War, which began in 1990 when the Rwandan Patriotic Front (RPF), a rebel group mainly composed of Tutsi refugees, invaded northern Rwanda from Uganda. Despite efforts to find a peaceful resolution through the Arusha Accords signed in 1993, the assassination of Hutu President Juvénal Habyarimana on April 6, 1994, led to the outbreak of mass killings the next day.

During the genocide, the majority of victims were killed in their own villages and towns by their neighbors, Hutu soldiers, police, and militias. Hutu gangs searched for victims in churches and schools, using machetes and rifles to murder them. Sexual violence was also widespread, with an estimated 250,000 to 500,000 women being raped.The international response to the genocide was limited, and no country intervened forcefully to stop the killings. The Rwandan Patriotic Front resumed the civil war and ultimately ended the genocide by capturing all government territory, forcing the government and perpetrators into Zaire (now the Democratic Republic of the Congo (Sullivan, 1994).

The aftermath of the genocide had significant and long-lasting effects.

In 1996, the Rwandan government launched an offensive into Zaire, starting the First Congo War and resulting in an estimated 200,000 deaths.

Today, Rwanda commemorates the genocide with two public holidays, and "genocide ideology" and "divisionism" are criminal offenses. The exact death toll remains a subject of debate, but the Constitution of Rwanda states that over 1 million people perished in the genocide (McDoom, 2020).

Seeking justice for the genocide in Rwanda has been a crucial and complex endeavor since the tragic events that occurred in 1994. The Rwandan genocide was a period of intense violence in which approximately 800,000 ethnic Tutsis and moderate Hutus were systematically killed over a span of about 100 days. The aftermath of such a horrific event called for accountability, reconciliation, and healing.

Several approaches have been taken to pursue justice for the genocide:

1. International Criminal Tribunal for Rwanda (ICTR): In the aftermath of the genocide, the United Nations established the ICTR to prosecute individuals responsible for the atrocities committed during the

genocide. The tribunal was based in Arusha, Tanzania, and played a significant role in bringing some of the key perpetrators to justice. It aimed to address not only the crimes committed but also the root causes of the genocide.

2. Community-Based Gacaca Courts: In addition to the international tribunal, Rwanda established a unique community-based justice system known as the Gacaca courts. These courts were designed to handle the large number of cases resulting from the genocide and promote truth-telling, reconciliation, and healing at the local level. The Gacaca courts involved the community in the process and encouraged confession and forgiveness.

3. National Unity and Reconciliation Commission (NURC): The NURC was established to promote unity and reconciliation among Rwandans, emphasizing the importance of healing and moving forward as a nation. It has worked to create spaces for dialogue and facilitated efforts to bridge divisions among the different ethnic groups in Rwanda.

4. International Collaboration: Seeking justice for the genocide in Rwanda has involved collaboration between the Rwandan government and international organizations, including NGOs and human rights groups. These collaborations have supported efforts in identifying perpetrators, providing assistance to survivors, and promoting accountability.

5. Dealing with Perpetrators Abroad: Many individuals suspected of participating in the genocide fled Rwanda and sought refuge in other countries. International efforts, such as extradition requests and trials in foreign jurisdictions, have been made to bring these individuals to justice.

6. Educational Initiatives: Addressing the legacy of the genocide has involved educational initiatives in Rwanda, aimed at promoting tolerance, understanding, and prevention of such atrocities in the future. These efforts have included revising the school curriculum to emphasize unity and reconciliation.

Seeking justice for the genocide in Rwanda has been a multifaceted process that requires ongoing commitment from both Rwandans and the international community. While significant progress has been made, challenges remain, and the quest for justice, reconciliation, and healing continues to be an essential aspect of Rwanda's journey toward a more peaceful and united society.

Sophie Nkirilene, who suffers from cholera, begs for help at the Kabumba camp on Aug. 6, 1994. DIXIE D. VEREEN, USA TODAY

CHAPTER NINE

The International Criminal Court (ICC) and Human Rights
The International Criminal Court (ICC) is a permanent
international tribunal based in The Hague, Netherlands. It
was established in 2002 through the multilateral Rome Statute
and is the first and only court with jurisdiction to prosecute
individuals for the most serious international crimes, such as
genocide, crimes against humanity, war crimes, and the crime
of aggression. The ICC operates independently and is separate
from the International Court of Justice, which deals with
disputes between states. The establishment of the ICC is
widely regarded as a significant advancement in the pursuit of
justice and human rights at the international level. It
represents an innovative approach to addressing and
prosecuting individuals responsible for grave international
crimes, regardless of their positions or status. By doing so, the
ICC seeks to hold perpetrators accountable and prevent future
atrocities.

International Criminal Court, The Hague.
| jbdodane/Flickr. Creative Commons (by-nc)

However, the ICC has faced criticism from various quarters. Some governments and civil society groups have raised objections to its jurisdiction, claiming that it may encroach upon national sovereignty. There have been accusations of bias, Eurocentrism, and racism in the court's operations and case selection. Additionally, concerns have been raised about the fairness of its trial procedures, leading to debates about its overall effectiveness. Despite these challenges and criticisms, the ICC remains an important institution in the global pursuit of justice and human rights. It plays a crucial role in addressing impunity for the most serious crimes and providing victims with a platform to seek justice and reparations. The ICC's work contributes to the deterrence of future crimes and fosters a culture of accountability for international crimes. However, ongoing efforts to address criticism and improve its functioning are necessary to enhance its legitimacy and effectiveness in the international community (Dancy, 2021).

Mandate of the International Criminal Court

The International Criminal Court (ICC) has jurisdiction to prosecute individuals for specific crimes listed in the Rome Statute, which include genocide, crimes against humanity, war crimes, and crimes of aggression.

1. Genocide: Genocide is defined in Article 6 of the Rome Statute as acts committed with the intent to destroy, in whole or in part, a national, ethnical, racial, or religious group. These acts include killing members of the group, causing serious bodily or mental harm, deliberately inflicting conditions of life to bring about physical destruction, imposing measures to prevent births within the group, and forcibly transferring children of the group to another group.

2. Crimes Against Humanity: Article 7 of the Rome Statute defines crimes against humanity as acts committed as part of a widespread or systematic attack against any civilian population, with knowledge of the attack. It includes a range of individual acts such as murder, enslavement, torture, rape, sexual slavery, persecution, enforced disappearance, apartheid, and other inhumane acts.

3. War Crimes: Article 8 of the Rome Statute defines war crimes depending on whether the armed conflict is international or non-international. It lists 74 war crimes, including grave breaches of the Geneva Conventions (applicable to international conflicts) and serious violations of Article 3 common to the Geneva Conventions (applicable to non-international conflicts). War crimes include acts like willful killing, torture, inhumane treatment, using prohibited weapons, attacking civilians, employing child soldiers, and more.

4. Crimes of Aggression: Crimes of aggression were added by an amendment to the Rome Statute and were activated in 2018. Article 8 bis defines crimes of aggression as the planning, preparation, initiation, or

execution of an act of aggression by a person in a position to direct the political or military action of a state. Acts of aggression include invasion, military occupation, annexation, bombardment, and other acts against the sovereignty, territorial integrity, or political independence of another state.

The ICC can only exercise jurisdiction over these crimes if they are committed on the territory of a state party to the Rome Statute or by a national of a state party. Additionally, the United Nations Security Council can refer situations involving these crimes to the ICC, even if the state involved is not a party to the Rome Statute. The Court's mandate is to bring justice to individuals responsible for these grave international crimes and to contribute to the prevention and deterrence of such crimes in the future (LeBor, 2011).

Trial History of the ICC

As of the latest available 23rd of July, 2023, the International Criminal Court (ICC) has conducted investigations and examinations in various countries and situations related to alleged war crimes and crimes against humanity. Here is a summary of the trial history and current status of some of these cases:

Trial History

I. Thomas Lubanga, Germain Katanga, and Mathieu Ngudjolo Chui were tried by the ICC. Lubanga and Katanga were convicted, while Chui was acquitted.

II. Jean-Pierre Bemba was convicted on counts of crimes against humanity and war crimes, including sexual violence. However, his convictions were later overturned by the Court's Appeal Chamber.

III. Trials are ongoing in the cases of Bosco Ntaganda in the DR Congo, the Bemba et al. case, and the Laurent Gbagbo-Blé Goudé trial in the Côte d'Ivoire situation.

IV.   The trial of Abdallah Banda in the Darfur, Sudan situation was scheduled to begin in 2014 but the start date was vacated.

V.   Charges against Dominic Ongwen of Uganda and Ahmad al-Faqi al-Mahdi of Mali have been confirmed, and both were awaiting their trials as of March 2020.

VI.   Two Uyghur activist groups filed a complaint with the ICC in July 2020, calling for an investigation of PRC officials for crimes against Uyghurs, including allegations of genocide.

Investigations and Preliminary Examinations

I.   The Office of the Prosecutor has opened investigations in several countries, including Afghanistan, the Central African Republic, Côte d'Ivoire, Darfur (Sudan), the Democratic Republic of the Congo, Kenya, Libya, Uganda, Bangladesh/Myanmar, Palestine, and Venezuela.

II.   The Office of the Prosecutor has conducted preliminary examinations in other situations, such as Bolivia, Colombia, Guinea, Iraq/United Kingdom, Nigeria, Georgia, Honduras, South Korea, Ukraine, and Venezuela.

III.   Preliminary investigations were closed in some cases, including Gabon, Honduras, registered vessels of Comoros, Greece, and Cambodia, South Korea, and Colombia for events since 1 July 2002.

The ICC's work is complex and faces challenges, including securing the arrest of fugitives and addressing criticism and questions about its jurisdiction, fairness, and effectiveness. Nevertheless, it represents a significant effort in seeking justice for individuals accused of committing grave international crimes and promoting accountability for such actions.

ICC Arrest warrant for Russian President Vladimir Putin over War in Ukraine

After the dissolution of the Soviet Union in 1991, Ukraine and Russia had close ties. Ukraine agreed to join the Treaty on the Non-Proliferation of Nuclear Weapons as a non-nuclear-weapon state, and in return, Russia, the United Kingdom, and the United States provided security assurances through the Budapest Memorandum, pledging to uphold Ukraine's territorial integrity and political independence.

However, in the years following the USSR's dissolution, several former Eastern Bloc countries joined NATO, leading to tensions with Russia.

The 2004 Ukrainian presidential election was controversial, with allegations of vote-rigging.

The Orange Revolution, a series of large peaceful protests, successfully challenged the initial election outcome and brought opposition candidate Viktor Yushchenko to power.

Russia accused the West of supporting these color revolutions in neighboring countries to undermine Russia's national security (Hall, 2022).

Deposed Ukrainian president Viktor Yanukovych.
AP FILE PHOTO

In 2008, Ukraine and Georgia sought to join NATO, but NATO members were divided on offering Membership Action Plans (MAPs) due to concerns about antagonizing Russia. Putin strongly opposed these bids. In 2010, Viktor Yanukovych became president of Ukraine, but his decision to reject the EU-Ukraine Association Agreement in favor of closer ties with Russia led to pro-European Union protests known as Euromaidan.

Following months of protests, Yanukovych fled the country, and an interim government was established. In response, Russia launched a military campaign in Crimea, leading to pro-Russian unrest in eastern regions of Ukraine.These events set the stage for the ongoing Russo-Ukrainian War, with Russia annexing Crimea and supporting pro-Russian separatists in eastern Ukraine.

The conflict has resulted in significant casualties, a refugee crisis, and international condemnation of Russia's actions. Tensions between Russia and Ukraine, as well as with the international community, remain high.

2022 Invasion

The Russian invasion of Ukraine began on February 24, 2022, when Russian President Vladimir Putin announced a "special military operation" to "demilitarize and denazify" Ukraine. Following the announcement, missiles and airstrikes hit various locations across Ukraine, including Kyiv, and a large ground invasion took place on multiple fronts. Russian attacks were launched from Belarus towards Kyiv (northern front), from Crimea (southern front), and from Luhansk and Donetsk (south-eastern front). Additionally, a north-eastern front was directed towards Kharkiv.

In response to the invasion, Ukrainian President Volodymyr Zelenskyy declared martial law and a general mobilization of all male Ukrainian citizens between 18 and 60 years old. Russian forces faced strong resistance and heavy losses in their advance towards Kyiv, leading to a stall in their progress in March. By April, Russian troops retreated from some areas and placed their forces in southern and eastern Ukraine under the command of General Aleksandr Dvornikov. However, on April 19, Russia launched a renewed attack extending from Kharkiv to Donetsk and Luhansk.

Throughout the conflict, both military and civilian targets were bombed by Russian forces far from the frontline. The war led to the largest refugee and humanitarian crisis within Europe since the Yugoslav Wars in the 1990s, with over a million refugees reported within the first week of the invasion and over 7.4 million refugees by September 24, 2022.

Ukrainian forces launched counteroffensives in the south in August and in the northeast in September. On September 30, 2022, Russia annexed four oblasts of Ukraine that it had partially conquered during the invasion, an action that was internationally unrecognized and condemned.

The invasion was widely condemned as a war of aggression, leading to the imposition of sanctions on Russia by many countries and the provision of humanitarian and military aid to Ukraine.

In response to conscription efforts in Russia, an international push was made to allow asylum for Russians fleeing conscription.

As of February 2023, The New York Times estimates that the number of Russian troops killed and wounded in Ukraine is approaching 200,000. The conflict remains ongoing and has had significant humanitarian and geopolitical implications.

Members of the Wagner Group military
company guard an area standing in front
of a tank in a street in Rostov-on-Don, Russia,
Saturday, June 24, 2023
(Vasily Deryugin, Kommersant
Publishing House via AP, File)

Indictment by the ICC for War crimes
On March 17th 2023, the International Criminal Court (ICC) has issued an arrest warrant for Russian President Vladimir Putin in relation to the forced deportation of children from Ukraine to Russia, where many have been adopted by Russian families. The ICC has determined that there are reasonable grounds to believe that Mr. Putin bears individual criminal responsibility for these child abductions, which are recognized as a crime under the Rome Statute that established the court.
Overall, the ICC arrest warrant for Vladimir Putin may serve as a symbolic statement of the court's stance on the alleged crimes, but its practical impact on Putin's legal situation is currently limited due to the factors mentioned above.
African leaders as easy targets for the ICC

The establishment of the International Criminal Court (ICC) in 2002 was seen as a noble effort to address international crimes such as genocide and crimes against humanity. However, over time, the court has faced criticism and lack of trust among some African leaders and the public. One major concern is the perception that the ICC is biased against Africans, as all its investigations and cases so far have been focused on African countries. Critics argue that the ICC's disproportionate focus on Africa raises questions about its credibility and impartiality. They point out that other regions with serious human rights violations, such as the Middle East and Syria, have not been subject to ICC investigations due to lack of UN Security Council intervention. Supporters of the ICC contend that its jurisdiction in Africa is a result of practical factors, including requests or referrals from African governments themselves. Many African states signed the Rome Statute, giving the ICC jurisdiction, while some major countries, such as the United States, did not ratify the treaty.

The ICC's pursuit of senior government officials, like Sudanese President Omar al-Bashir and Kenyan President Uhuru Kenyatta, has further strained relations with African leaders. Some African leaders have criticized the court only when it goes after heads of state, while showing little concern for ICC prosecutions against rebel leaders or militia groups. The situation in South Africa, where Bashir attended an African Union summit and escaped despite an ICC arrest warrant, illustrates the complexity and challenges the court faces in enforcing its decisions.

Despite the criticisms and controversies, the ICC continues its work, aiming to bring justice to victims of international crimes. However, the optics of the court's focus on Africa have significantly impacted its credibility on the continent and beyond. Rebuilding trust and addressing concerns of bias will remain critical for the ICC's effectiveness and legitimacy in the future (Adam, 2015).

ICC's jurisdiction over human rights violations in Africa

The International Criminal Court (ICC) is a permanent international court established to prosecute individuals for the most serious crimes of international concern, such as genocide, war crimes, crimes against humanity, and the crime of aggression. The ICC's jurisdiction is not limited to any specific region or continent, but rather it is a global court with the authority to investigate and prosecute crimes committed anywhere in the world.

Regarding human rights violations in Africa, the ICC has been involved in investigating and prosecuting cases related to serious crimes in various African countries. It's essential to note that the ICC's involvement in Africa has been a subject of debate and criticism, with some African leaders and governments expressing concerns about perceived bias and disproportionate focus on the continent.

Several high-profile cases related to human rights violations in Africa that have come under the ICC's jurisdiction include:

1. Democratic Republic of the Congo (DRC): The ICC has investigated and prosecuted various cases of war crimes and crimes against humanity in the DRC, including those committed by armed groups and individuals during armed conflicts.

2. Uganda: The ICC has been involved in cases related to the Lord's Resistance Army (LRA) insurgency in Uganda, targeting individuals accused of committing war crimes and crimes against humanity.

3. Sudan/Darfur: The ICC has issued arrest warrants for high-ranking Sudanese officials, including former President Omar al-Bashir, for their alleged involvement in crimes committed during the conflict in Darfur.

4. Kenya: The ICC investigated post-election violence in Kenya in 2007-2008, leading to charges against high-ranking politicians. However, the cases were later dropped due to various challenges faced during the proceedings.

5. Central African Republic (CAR): The ICC has investigated and prosecuted individuals accused of committing crimes in the CAR, including acts of violence during the ongoing civil conflict.
6. Liberia: The ICC has played a role in addressing human rights violations in Liberia, particularly during the country's civil wars. The court has investigated and prosecuted individuals alleged to have committed serious crimes, contributing to efforts for accountability and justice in the country.
7. Sierra Leone: The ICC has been involved in cases related to the Sierra Leone Civil War, which occurred between 1991 and 2002. The court has prosecuted individuals for war crimes, crimes against humanity, and other serious offenses committed during the conflict.
8. Rwanda: While the International Criminal Tribunal for Rwanda (ICTR) had primary jurisdiction over cases related to the Rwandan genocide in 1994, the ICC has also investigated and prosecuted individuals accused of committing crimes within its mandate related to the post-genocide period.

It is important to recognize that the ICC's jurisdiction is complementary to national jurisdictions, meaning that it steps in only when national authorities are unwilling or unable to prosecute such crimes themselves. Additionally, the ICC can also act when the UN Security Council refers a case to the Court. Criticism of the ICC's focus on Africa includes allegations of bias, selective targeting, and interference in the internal affairs of African countries. Proponents of the ICC argue that the court's role is to hold perpetrators of serious international crimes accountable and that its involvement in Africa is due to the prevalence of such crimes in the region.

It's crucial to approach discussions about the ICC's role in Africa with nuance, considering the complexity of the situations, the Court's mandate, and the challenges of bringing justice to victims of grave human rights violations.

Criticisms and challenges faced by the ICC in Africa

In her Bram Fischer Memorial Lecture, UN Human Rights chief Navi Pillay praised the work of human rights defenders in Africa, highlighting their crucial role in upholding rights and democratic principles. These defenders advocate for education, equality, freedom of speech, and participation in decision-making processes. They also campaign against the exploitation of natural resources and demand accountability from governments and institutions.

Despite their important contributions, human rights defenders in Africa face challenges, including harassment, death threats, and attacks.

Pillay acknowledged their courage in standing up against adversity, drawing parallels to the bravery of Bram Fischer, a renowned South African human rights lawyer and anti-apartheid activist. Pillay also addressed the issue of counter-terrorism measures, emphasizing the need for such laws to be assessed against international human rights standards to prevent misuse and ensure they are proportionate and effective. Regarding elections in Africa, Pillay emphasized that they offer a critical opportunity for people to exercise their civil and political rights. However, elections can also be a sensitive moment, potentially leading to violence or human rights violations. The Office of the High Commissioner for Human Rights is actively involved in electoral monitoring in various African countries. In conclusion, Pillay stressed the importance of democracy as an ongoing process, closely tied to human rights. She advocated for inclusive societies where everyone's voice is heard and contributions are valued (Pillay, 2013).

The International Criminal Court (ICC) has faced several criticisms and challenges specific to its operations in Africa. Some of the key criticisms and challenges include:

I. Geographic Bias: The most prominent criticism against the ICC in Africa is its perceived geographic bias. All of the court's investigations and cases have focused on African countries, leading to accusations of targeting African leaders disproportionately. This has fueled perceptions of an anti-African bias within the ICC.

II. Sovereignty Concerns: Some African countries have raised concerns about the ICC's jurisdiction and its potential encroachment on their national sovereignty. They argue that the court's interventions may interfere with their internal affairs and domestic legal processes.

III. Political Interference: The ICC's actions in Africa have been seen by some as politically motivated and influenced by powerful states. African leaders have accused the court of being used as a tool for political interests, particularly by Western nations.

IV. Cooperation Challenges: The ICC relies on cooperation from member states to execute its arrest warrants and gather evidence. Some African countries have been reluctant to cooperate with the court, making it difficult to execute arrest warrants and ensure accountability for suspects.

V. Peace Versus Justice Dilemma: The ICC's involvement in ongoing conflicts can create tensions between the pursuit of justice and the need for peace negotiations. Some critics argue that ICC investigations and prosecutions may hinder peace processes and reconciliation efforts.

VI. Limited Deterrence: Critics have raised concerns about the ICC's limited deterrence effect on potential perpetrators of international crimes in Africa. Perpetrators may believe they can avoid accountability, especially if they perceive the risk of ICC prosecution as low.

VII. Resource Imbalance: The ICC's focus on African cases has led to resource imbalances, with limited attention and resources allocated to cases in other regions. This has raised questions about the court's ability to address global justice concerns.

VIII. Lack of Local Ownership: Some argue that the ICC's approach may not sufficiently involve local communities and authorities in Africa. This lack of local ownership can affect the perceived legitimacy and effectiveness of the court's interventions.

IX. African Union Criticism: The African Union (AU) has been vocal in its criticism of the ICC's operations in Africa. The AU has accused the court of targeting African leaders and has called for immunity for sitting heads of state, which the ICC rejects.

X. Slow Pace of Justice: ICC trials can be lengthy and time-consuming, leading to delays in delivering justice and reparations for victims. The slow pace of proceedings may undermine the court's credibility and legitimacy in the eyes of affected communities.

Despite these criticisms and challenges, some African countries and civil society groups continue to support the ICC's role in pursuing accountability for serious international crimes and providing justice for victims. The ICC remains an essential institution in the fight against impunity for grave human rights violations. However, addressing these criticisms and engaging constructively with African states is crucial for the court to enhance its credibility and effectiveness on the continent.

Alfred Yekatom former Central
African militia leader, also known as "Colonel Rambo"
The Hague, Netherlands | AFP

CHAPTER TEN

Advancements and Setbacks in Human Rights

Advancements and setbacks in human rights have occurred throughout history and continue to shape the global landscape. Here are some examples of both:

Advancements in Human Rights

1. Universal Declaration of Human Rights (UDHR): Adopted by the United Nations General Assembly in 1948, the UDHR represents a significant milestone in the recognition and protection of human rights worldwide. It serves as a foundational document, guiding the development of international human rights law and inspiring national constitutions and laws.

2. Civil Rights Movement: The Civil Rights Movement in the United States during the 1950s and 1960s led to significant advancements in the recognition and protection of civil rights for African Americans. Key achievements included the Civil Rights Act of 1964 and the Voting Rights Act of 1965, which outlawed racial discrimination and ensured voting rights for all citizens.

3. Gender Equality: Progress has been made in promoting gender equality and women's rights. Advancements include the Convention on the Elimination of All Forms of Discrimination against Women (CEDAW) and increased representation of women in leadership positions globally.

4. Rights of Persons with Disabilities: The adoption of the United Nations Convention on the Rights of Persons with Disabilities (CRPD) in 2006 marked a crucial step in promoting and protecting the rights of persons with disabilities worldwide.

Setbacks in Human Rights

1. Armed Conflicts and Human Rights Violations: Ongoing armed conflicts in various regions have led to widespread human rights abuses, including war crimes, genocide, and crimes against humanity.

2. Rise of Authoritarianism: Some countries have experienced a decline in human rights protections due to the rise of authoritarian regimes, which curtail civil liberties, suppress political opposition, and limit freedom of expression.

3. Discrimination and Marginalization: Discrimination based on race, ethnicity, religion, and other factors remains prevalent in many societies, leading to

marginalization and denial of basic rights to certain groups.

4. Refugee Crisis: The global refugee crisis has highlighted the challenges in protecting the rights of displaced persons, with many facing unsafe conditions, lack of access to basic services, and inadequate legal protections.

5. Surveillance and Privacy Concerns: Advancements in technology have raised concerns about privacy rights and government surveillance, with potential implications for freedom of speech and individual liberties.

Addressing these setbacks and promoting human rights advancements requires collective efforts from governments, civil society organizations, international institutions, and individuals. Continued advocacy, legal action, and awareness-raising are essential to protect and promote the fundamental rights and dignity of all individuals worldwide.

Success stories in promoting human rights in Africa

There have been several success stories in promoting human rights in Africa over the years. While challenges persist, progress has been made in various areas. Here are some success stories:

I. The End of Apartheid in South Africa: One of the most significant human rights achievements in Africa was the end of apartheid in South Africa. Through nonviolent resistance and international pressure, apartheid was dismantled, and South Africa transitioned to a multiracial democracy in the early 1990s, paving the way for greater human rights protection and equality.

II.	The Campaign to End Female Genital Mutilation (FGM): Many African countries have made progress in combatting female genital mutilation, a harmful traditional practice that violates human rights and poses serious health risks to women and girls. Through advocacy, awareness campaigns, and legal reforms, the prevalence of FGM has decreased in several countries.

III.	The Establishment of Human Rights Institutions: Several African countries have established human rights institutions such as national human rights commissions and ombudsman offices. These institutions play a crucial role in promoting and protecting human rights, monitoring violations, and providing redress to victims.

IV.	The Fight against Child Marriage: Many African countries have taken steps to address child marriage, recognizing that it violates the rights of young girls and perpetuates a cycle of poverty and discrimination. Legal reforms and awareness campaigns have led to a decline in child marriage rates in some regions.

V.	Access to Education: Some African countries have made significant progress in improving access to education, especially for girls and marginalized communities. Education is a fundamental human right, and efforts to promote inclusive and quality education contribute to broader human rights advancements.

VI.	Peacebuilding Efforts: Peacebuilding initiatives in various African countries have contributed to the protection and promotion of human rights. Peace agreements and reconciliation processes have helped to address human rights violations and create a more stable and inclusive society.

VII.	Economic and Social Rights Advancements: Some African countries have made progress in addressing economic and social rights, including access to healthcare, housing, and social welfare programs. These efforts contribute to reducing poverty and inequality.

Gender equality and Women's rights in Africa

Gender equality and women's rights in Africa have been areas of significant concern and advocacy for several decades. While progress has been made, there are still many challenges that hinder the full realization of gender equality and the protection of women's rights on the continent.

Gender equality is a fundamental human rights principle that advocates for equal access to resources, opportunities, and decision-making regardless of gender. It goes beyond merely ensuring equal representation and seeks to value and recognize the diverse behaviors, aspirations, and needs of individuals irrespective of their gender identity. Gender equality is a goal that encompasses both women's rights and men's rights, aiming to create a fair and just society where all genders have equal opportunities to thrive.

Achieving gender equality involves challenging and eliminating harmful practices and oppressive tactics that disproportionately affect women and girls, such as sex trafficking, femicide, gender wage gap, and wartime sexual violence. It also addresses the social and cultural stereotypes that have historically relegated women to roles as primary caregivers and homemakers, limiting their access to property ownership, education, and employment opportunities (LeMonyne, 2011).

UNICEF emphasizes that gender equality does not imply that all individuals should be treated exactly alike, but rather that they should have equal rights, resources, and protections. It acknowledges the unique needs and experiences of different genders and seeks to ensure that everyone can live without discrimination and enjoy the same opportunities for personal and professional growth.

On a global scale, gender equality is recognized as a crucial component of sustainable development. The United Nations has included it as one of the seventeen Sustainable Development Goals (SDG 5), highlighting its significance in building a more inclusive and equitable world. Despite international agreements affirming gender equality as a human right, various challenges persist, such as gender-based poverty, illiteracy, limited access to property and credit, and domestic violence (Fineman, 2000).

To achieve gender equality, it is essential to address systemic inequalities, promote women's empowerment, challenge harmful stereotypes, and encourage the active participation of women in all spheres of life, including politics, education, and the economy. This requires not only policy changes but also a shift in societal attitudes and norms towards more inclusive and gender-neutral perspectives. By striving for gender equality, societies can harness the full potential of all individuals and foster a more prosperous and harmonious future for everyone (UNFPA, 2015).

Gender equality envisions a world where individuals of all genders are treated equally in all aspects of society, without discrimination based on their gender. This vision encompasses social, economic, political, and cultural spheres, seeking to eliminate existing gender-based disparities and ensure that all individuals have the same opportunities and rights, regardless of their gender identity.

The concept of gender equality is deeply rooted in human rights principles.

The United Nations Universal Declaration of Human Rights recognizes it as one of its objectives, emphasizing the importance of upholding equal rights and opportunities for men and women. Additionally, gender equality is central to the achievement of the Millennium Development Goals, with a specific focus on empowering women and promoting their rights. Gender equality is not limited to women's rights; it extends to promoting fairness and inclusivity for people of all genders. It addresses various issues, including the gender wage gap, gender-based violence, and limited access to education and healthcare, which have historically affected women more severely.

Promoting gender equality is essential for fostering economic development and sustainable growth in all nations. It recognizes that empowering women economically and socially leads to improved overall well-being and productivity. By providing women with equal opportunities to participate in the workforce and receive fair pay for their work, societies can harness the full potential of their human resources.

While progress has been made in advancing gender equality globally, challenges persist, particularly in developing countries.

The United Nations continues to work towards promoting gender equality and creating a sustainable living environment for all nations. This includes efforts to address economic struggles and implement policies that bridge gender gaps in various sectors.

Achieving gender equality requires a collective commitment from governments, organizations, and individuals. It involves challenging societal norms and stereotypes, promoting inclusive policies, and ensuring that all individuals have equal access to education, healthcare, and economic opportunities. By striving for gender equality, the world can move closer to realizing the vision of a fair, just, and prosperous society for everyone (World Bank, 2006).

Women's rights in Africa have been a significant focus of attention, advocacy, and progress over the years. While the status of women's rights varies across the continent due to its diverse cultural, social, economic, and political landscapes, there have been notable advancements as well as persistent challenges.

Legal Reforms: Many African countries have made strides in enacting legal reforms to protect and promote women's rights. These include laws addressing gender-based violence, sexual harassment, and discrimination. For instance, several countries have passed legislation to criminalize female genital mutilation (FGM) and child marriage.

1. Gender Equality Policies: Some African governments have adopted policies aimed at promoting gender equality and women's empowerment. These policies often focus on increasing women's participation in decision-making, education, and the workforce.

2. Education: Progress has been made in improving access to education for girls and women in Africa. Efforts have been made to reduce gender disparities in school enrollment, and initiatives like girls' education programs have been implemented to encourage girls to stay in school.

3. Healthcare: There have been efforts to improve women's access to healthcare services, including reproductive healthcare. Initiatives to reduce maternal

mortality and improve access to family planning have been pursued in various countries.

4. Economic Empowerment: Programs to promote women's economic empowerment, such as access to credit and entrepreneurship training, have been implemented to enhance their participation in economic activities.

5. Ending Gender-Based Violence: There is a growing recognition of the need to address gender-based violence, including domestic violence, sexual assault, and trafficking of women and girls. Many countries have adopted laws and established support services for survivors.

6. Women in Politics: Progress has been made in increasing women's representation in political leadership roles, both at the national and local levels. Some countries have introduced quotas or affirmative action measures to ensure greater female political participation.

However, despite these advancements, numerous challenges persist:

1. Cultural Norms and Traditions: Deep-rooted cultural norms and traditional practices often perpetuate gender inequalities, particularly in rural and conservative areas. Practices like FGM, child marriage, and unequal inheritance rights are still prevalent in some regions.

2. Violence and Discrimination: Gender-based violence remains a significant concern, and many women continue to face discrimination in various spheres of life, limiting their opportunities and potential

3. Access to Education: While progress has been made in improving girls' access to education, there are still disparities, particularly in remote and marginalized communities.

4. Healthcare Disparities: Women in certain regions may face challenges in accessing quality healthcare services, especially in maternal health and reproductive care.

5. Economic Disparities: Women often face barriers to economic opportunities, including limited access to credit, land ownership, and decent-paying jobs.

6. Political Underrepresentation: Despite progress in increasing women's representation in politics, women are still underrepresented in many decision-making bodies and face barriers to active political participation.

7. Conflict and Instability: Women and girls are disproportionately affected by conflicts and humanitarian crises, facing violence, displacement, and exploitation.

Addressing these challenges requires sustained efforts from governments, civil society organizations, and international partners. It involves addressing cultural norms, enforcing existing laws, investing in education and healthcare, promoting economic opportunities, and empowering women to participate fully in all aspects of society. By promoting and protecting women's rights, Africa can unleash the potential of half of its population and contribute to more inclusive and sustainable development across the continent.

As a finale to their last meeting at Hunter College, the Sub-commission on the Status of Women hold a press conference in the delegates lounge of the gym building. Left to Right: Angela Jurdak (Lebanon), Fryderyka Kalinowski (Poland), Bodgil Begtrup (Denmark), Minerva Bernardino (Dominican Republic), and Hansa Mehta (India), delegates to the Sub-commission on the Status of Women, New York, May 1946. UN Photo

Campaign against Female Genital Mutilation (FGM) in Africa

Female Genital Mutilation (FGM), also known as female genital cutting, is a harmful traditional practice that involves the cutting or removal of some or all of the external female genitalia. It is prevalent in some countries in Africa, Asia, and the Middle East, as well as within their diasporas.

FGM is typically performed by traditional circumcisers using blades and is conducted from days after birth to puberty and even beyond. UNICEF estimates that as of 2023, at least 200 million girls and women in 31 countries have undergone FGM (Nussbaum, 199).

The procedures of FGM vary depending on the country or ethnic group and can include different levels of genital tissue removal. They range from the removal of the clitoral hood or clitoral glans to the excision of the inner and outer labia with the closure of the vulva, known as infibulation. In infibulation, a small hole is left for the passage of urine and menstrual fluid, while the vagina is opened for intercourse and childbirth. FGM is deeply rooted in gender inequality and attempts to control women's sexuality. It is often seen as a source of honor and a way to ensure purity, modesty, and beauty.

Many practitioners fear that failing to have their daughters and granddaughters cut will lead to social exclusion. The practice of FGM has severe health consequences.

The adverse effects can include recurrent infections, difficulty urinating and passing menstrual flow, chronic pain, the development of cysts, infertility, complications during childbirth, and fatal bleeding. It is essential to note that there are no known health benefits associated with FGM. Efforts to combat FGM have been ongoing since the 1970s, aiming to persuade practitioners to abandon the practice. Many countries have outlawed or restricted FGM, but enforcement of laws remains a challenge. Since 2010, the United Nations has called upon healthcare providers to stop performing all forms of FGM, including reinfibulation after childbirth and symbolic "nicking" of the clitoral hood (Abdulcadir etal, 2011). Critics of the opposition to FGM, particularly among some anthropologists, have raised questions about cultural relativism and the universality of human rights. However, the movement against FGM is driven by the recognition of the practice's severe human rights violations and the efforts to protect the health, well-being, and dignity of women and girls. It is an ongoing struggle to eradicate FGM and promote gender equality and the rights of women and girls around the world.

Campaign for Poverty Eradication, Universal Basic Education fight against diseases and economic inequality in Africa (Shell-Duncan, 2008).

FGM awareness session run by the African Union Mission to Somalia at the Walalah Biylooley refugee camp, Mogadishu, 2014

AU UN IST PHOTO / David Mutua

Persistent challenges and obstacles to progress

It is essential to acknowledge that promoting human rights is an ongoing process, and challenges persist in many areas. However, these success stories demonstrate that progress is possible with collective efforts, political will, and the dedication of human rights activists and organizations in Africa.

Despite significant advancements in human rights, persistent challenges and obstacles continue to impede progress in ensuring universal protection and respect for human rights. Some of these challenges include:

1. Armed Conflicts and Violence: Ongoing armed conflicts, civil wars, and violence in various regions result in serious human rights violations, including civilian casualties, displacement, sexual violence, and recruitment of child soldiers.

2. Discrimination and Marginalization: Discrimination based on race, ethnicity, religion, gender, sexual orientation, and other factors continues to marginalize vulnerable populations, denying them equal access to opportunities and basic rights.

3. Authoritarian Regimes and Repression: The rise of authoritarian regimes in some countries has led to increased repression of political dissent, freedom of expression, and civil liberties, hindering the protection of human rights.

4. Economic Inequality: Economic disparities and poverty are major obstacles to the realization of human rights. Many individuals lack access to basic necessities, such as healthcare, education, housing, and clean water, which affects their overall well-being and dignity.

5. Migration and Refugee Crises: The increase in migration and refugee crises exposes vulnerable populations to exploitation, human trafficking, and violations of their rights during their journey and upon arrival in host countries.

6. Climate Change and Environmental Rights: Climate change poses significant threats to human rights, including the right to life, health, and access to resources. Vulnerable communities, especially in developing countries, bear the brunt of environmental degradation.

7. Cybersecurity and Digital Rights: Advances in technology have given rise to new challenges concerning privacy, surveillance, and freedom of

expression. Government surveillance and cyberattacks may infringe on individuals' digital rights and privacy.

8. Impunity and Lack of Accountability: Perpetrators of human rights violations often go unpunished due to weak legal systems, corruption, and lack of political will to address past and ongoing atrocities.

9. Backlash against Human Rights: In some countries, there is a growing backlash against human rights principles and institutions, with governments openly challenging human rights norms and undermining international cooperation.

10. Cultural Relativism: The concept of cultural relativism sometimes hinders the implementation of universal human rights standards, as some argue that certain cultural practices or beliefs should take precedence over human rights principles.

Addressing these persistent challenges requires sustained efforts from governments, civil society, international organizations, and individuals. Advocacy, education, strengthened legal frameworks, and the promotion of a human rights-based approach in policymaking are essential to overcoming these obstacles and advancing human rights for all.

Role of civil society, NGOs, and grassroots movements in Africa

Civil society, non-governmental organizations (NGOs), and grassroots movements play crucial roles in shaping and influencing African societies and promoting various aspects of human rights, democracy, and social development. Their contributions are significant and multifaceted:

I.   Advocacy and Awareness: Civil society organizations and grassroots movements are at the forefront of advocacy efforts, raising awareness about human rights issues, social injustices, and the needs of marginalized communities. They work to mobilize public support, foster a sense of solidarity, and engage in dialogue with governments and international bodies to push for policy changes and legal reforms.

II. Monitoring and Reporting: NGOs and civil society groups serve as independent watchdogs, monitoring and documenting human rights violations, corruption, and abuses of power. Through their reports and documentation, they can shed light on issues that might otherwise go unnoticed and hold governments and institutions accountable for their actions.

III. Service Provision: Many NGOs and grassroots movements are actively involved in providing essential services to vulnerable populations, such as access to education, healthcare, clean water, and social support. They often fill gaps in government services, ensuring that human rights are upheld and basic needs are met.

IV. Capacity Building and Empowerment: These organizations work to empower local communities and individuals, especially marginalized groups, by providing them with skills, knowledge, and resources to advocate for their rights and interests. This empowerment helps foster self-sufficiency and long-term development.

V. Peacebuilding and Conflict Resolution: Civil society plays a vital role in promoting peace and reconciliation in conflict-affected areas. NGOs and grassroots movements facilitate dialogue, promote tolerance, and work towards sustainable peace through community engagement and mediation.

VI. Environmental Protection: Many NGOs in Africa focus on environmental conservation and sustainable development. They work to address environmental issues, climate change, and natural resource management, ensuring that the rights of present and future generations are protected.

VII. Electoral Monitoring and Governance: During elections, civil society organizations often monitor the electoral process to ensure transparency, fairness, and credibility. They promote good governance, accountability, and the rule of law, contributing to democratic processes.

VIII. Legal Aid and Human Rights Protection: NGOs and civil society groups provide legal aid and support to victims of human rights violations, helping them seek justice and redress. They often partner with legal experts to pursue cases before domestic and international courts.

Overall, civil society, NGOs, and grassroots movements in Africa play vital roles in advocating for human rights, promoting social justice, and contributing to sustainable development. Their efforts complement and sometimes challenge government initiatives, ensuring that the voices of ordinary people are heard, and human rights are upheld.

CHAPTER ELEVEN

Reflections and Future Prospects
Reflections

Looking back, the advancements and setbacks in human rights in Africa have been both inspiring and challenging. There have been significant strides in promoting human rights, democracy, and social development in various countries across the continent. Civil society, non-governmental organizations, and grassroots movements have played crucial roles in advocating for human rights, raising awareness about issues, and holding governments accountable for their actions.

One of the notable success stories is the work of human rights defenders in Africa who have stood firm against threats, harassment, and attacks to protect human rights. Their efforts have been instrumental in pushing for positive changes and making a difference in the lives of marginalized communities. Additionally, the involvement of civil society in monitoring elections, promoting good governance, and advocating for peace and reconciliation has contributed to democratic processes and sustainable peace in conflict-affected regions.

However, there have also been setbacks and challenges. Human rights defenders in Africa continue to face risks and dangers, and some governments have been criticized for compromising human rights in the name of national security or counter-terrorism measures. The focus of international human rights bodies on African states has raised concerns about bias and a lack of attention to human rights violations in other regions.

Future Prospects

Looking ahead, there are several key areas where Africa's human rights landscape can be strengthened:

I. Strengthening National Institutions: African governments should work towards enhancing the capacity and independence of national human rights institutions, ensuring they have the resources and mandate to effectively protect and promote human rights.

II. Bridging the Gap Between Legislation and Implementation: There is a need to bridge the gap between existing human rights laws and their implementation on the ground. Governments should take concrete actions to enforce human rights protections and ensure that laws are effectively enforced.

III. Addressing Socio-Economic Rights: While there have been improvements in civil and political rights, socio-economic rights, such as access to education, healthcare, and housing, still need greater attention. Governments and civil society should collaborate to address issues of poverty, inequality, and social exclusion.

IV. Strengthening Regional and International Collaboration: African countries should continue to engage with regional and international human rights bodies to benefit from their expertise and support in promoting and protecting human rights.

V. Emphasizing Preventive Measures: Proactive measures should be taken to prevent human rights violations before they occur. This includes addressing the root causes of conflicts and promoting dialogue and tolerance among diverse communities.

VI. Leveraging Technology and Social Media: Utilizing technology and social media can amplify human rights advocacy, raise awareness, and mobilize public support for human rights causes.

By addressing these challenges and working collaboratively, Africa can continue its journey towards greater respect for human rights, social justice, and inclusive development. Civil society, NGOs, and grassroots movements will remain pivotal in shaping this future, advocating for the rights of all individuals, and building societies where everyone's voice counts.

Assessment of the UDHR's impact on human rights in Africa

The UDHR has had a considerable impact on human rights in Africa, serving as a benchmark for human rights principles and norms in both theory and practice. While the UDHR is not legally binding, it has been instrumental in shaping customary international law through state practice and opinio juris. Many African countries have ratified international human rights treaties, including the Human Rights Covenants, which amplify the UDHR.

The UDHR has been incorporated into the constitutions of African countries in various ways. Some countries have explicitly reaffirmed the principles of the UDHR in their preambles or operative parts. Others have referred to the UDHR as an integral part of their constitutions. Additionally, numerous constitutional guarantees in Africa's legal instruments align with the principles of the UDHR, reflecting its influence on constitutional engineering. African regional and sub-regional legal instruments often invoke the UDHR in their preambles and substantive provisions. For example, the Charter of the OAU (Organization of African Unity) and the Constitutive Act of the AU (African Union) reaffirmed adherence to the UDHR and principles of international cooperation. The African Charter on Human and Peoples' Rights references 18 of the 27 specific rights guaranteed in the UDHR.

Courts in various jurisdictions across Africa have also recognized the formative impact of the UDHR in shaping customary rules.

In some cases, the UDHR has been directly referred to in legal proceedings to address alleged human rights violations. Despite its impact, challenges persist in fully realizing the principles of the UDHR in Africa. Socioeconomic inequalities, weak enforcement mechanisms, cultural relativism arguments, and inconsistent state practice have hindered its complete implementation. However, the UDHR's influence remains significant in advocating for human rights protection and guiding legal and policy developments in the region. Overall, the UDHR has played a crucial role in shaping human rights discourse and practices in Africa, acting as a catalyst for the human rights movement and inspiring human rights defenders to advocate for social justice, equality, and fundamental freedoms. While progress has been made, ongoing efforts are necessary to address challenges and advance human rights in the continent (Udombana, 2023).

The impact of the Universal Declaration of Human Rights (UDHR) on human rights in Africa has been significant but also subject to challenges and limitations. The UDHR, adopted in 1948, provided a universal framework for human rights principles and served as a catalyst for the human rights movement worldwide. In Africa, the UDHR played a crucial role in shaping human rights discourse and practices, but its full realization faced various obstacles:

I. Positive Impact on Human Rights Discourse: The UDHR introduced universal human rights norms and values to African societies, encouraging discussions and debates on human rights issues. It influenced the development of regional and national human rights instruments in Africa, such as the African Charter on Human and Peoples' Rights and other regional protocols.

II. Legitimizing Human Rights Norms: The UDHR acted as a legitimizing force for human rights principles in African countries. Governments and civil society groups in Africa have often used the UDHR to advocate for human rights protection and hold states accountable for human rights violations.

III. Mobilization and Advocacy: The UDHR inspired human rights defenders in Africa to campaign for social justice, equality, and the protection of fundamental freedoms. Human rights activists have drawn on the UDHR's principles to advocate for marginalized and vulnerable groups, leading to positive changes in some instances.

IV. Challenges to Implementation: Despite its aspirational value, the UDHR faced challenges in implementation in Africa. Some African states struggled to fully align their domestic laws and practices with the principles outlined in the UDHR, leading to persistent human rights abuses in various regions.

V. Cultural and Relativist Critiques: The universality of human rights, as advocated by the UDHR, faced criticism in Africa based on cultural relativism arguments. Some critics argued that certain human rights principles might conflict with local customs, traditions, and religious beliefs, leading to resistance in implementing certain rights.

VI. Socioeconomic Inequalities: Many African countries continue to grapple with poverty, inequality, and political instability, which have hindered the full realization of human rights. Economic and social rights outlined in the UDHR, such as the right to education, health, and adequate standard of living, remain challenging to achieve in some parts of Africa.

VII. Weak Enforcement Mechanisms: The lack of robust enforcement mechanisms for international human rights standards has limited the effectiveness of the UDHR in Africa. Regional human rights bodies, such as the African Commission on Human and Peoples'

Rights, have made progress, but challenges remain in ensuring prompt and effective remedies for human rights violations.

In conclusion, the UDHR has undoubtedly had a significant impact on human rights in Africa by introducing universal human rights norms and inspiring activism. However, challenges in implementation, cultural relativism debates, socioeconomic inequalities, and weak enforcement mechanisms have limited its full realization. Continuous efforts by governments, civil society, and international organizations are necessary to address these challenges and advance human rights in Africa.

The influence of African human rights perspectives on international law

African human rights perspectives have had a significant impact on the development and interpretation of international law. Over the years, African countries and scholars have played a crucial role in shaping the discourse on human rights within the international community. Some of the key ways in which African perspectives have influenced international law include:

I. The African Charter on Human and Peoples' Rights: Adopted in 1981, the African Charter is a regional human rights treaty that specifically reflects the social, cultural, and economic context of the African continent. It recognizes not only individual rights but also collective rights, known as "peoples' rights," which emphasize the rights of communities and groups. This innovative approach to human rights has contributed to the evolution of international law to recognize the importance of collective rights.

II. Expanded Notions of Rights: African human rights perspectives have emphasized the interconnectedness of civil, political, economic, social, and cultural rights. This holistic understanding of human rights, known as the indivisibility and interdependence of rights, has been influential in the development of international human rights law, moving away from a narrow focus on civil and political rights to encompass economic, social, and cultural rights as well.

III. Women's Rights: African countries have been at the forefront of advancing women's rights within the international human rights framework. The Protocol to the African Charter on Human and Peoples' Rights on the Rights of Women in Africa (Maputo Protocol), adopted in 2003, is a groundbreaking treaty that addresses issues such as violence against women, harmful practices, and discrimination. It has inspired similar initiatives at the global level and strengthened the protection of women's rights in international law.

IV. Protection of Indigenous Peoples' Rights: African perspectives have contributed to advancing the rights of indigenous peoples within international law. African countries played a key role in the adoption of the United Nations Declaration on the Rights of Indigenous Peoples in 2007, which recognizes the rights of indigenous peoples to their lands, resources, and self-determination.

V. Reinterpretation of Universal Human Rights Principles: African scholars and advocates have engaged in critical discussions on the universality of human rights, advocating for the contextualization of human rights principles to the specific needs and challenges of African societies. This has enriched the dialogue on cultural relativism versus universalism in human rights.

VI. Regional Human Rights Systems: The African human rights system, including the African Commission on Human and Peoples' Rights and the African Court on Human and Peoples' Rights, has contributed to the implementation and enforcement of human rights standards on the continent. These regional mechanisms have served as models for other regional human rights systems around the world.

In conclusion, African human rights perspectives have significantly influenced international law, enriching the understanding of human rights, advocating for the protection of vulnerable groups, and contributing to the evolution of human rights norms and mechanisms. The African continent continues to play a crucial role in shaping the global human rights agenda and promoting the protection of human rights for all.

Ongoing efforts to strengthen human rights protection in Africa

Efforts to strengthen human rights protection in Africa are ongoing and involve various actors, including African governments, regional organizations, civil society, and international partners. Some key initiatives and strategies aimed at enhancing human rights protection in Africa include:

I. African Charter on Human and Peoples' Rights Implementation: African countries continue to work towards full implementation of the African Charter on Human and Peoples' Rights. This involves aligning domestic laws and policies with the provisions of the Charter, as well as establishing mechanisms for reporting, monitoring, and redressing human rights violations.

II. Strengthening Regional Human Rights Mechanisms: The African Commission on Human and Peoples' Rights and the African Court on Human and Peoples' Rights play essential roles in promoting human rights in Africa. Efforts are being made to enhance their effectiveness, capacity, and accessibility to individuals and communities seeking justice for human rights violations.

III. National Human Rights Institutions (NHRIs): Many African countries have established NHRIs as independent bodies responsible for promoting and protecting human rights at the national level. These institutions serve as important bridges between the government, civil society, and the international human rights community.

IV. Combatting Impunity: Addressing impunity for human rights violations is a priority in Africa. This includes efforts to investigate and prosecute those responsible for human rights abuses, particularly in conflict-affected regions. The establishment of special tribunals and hybrid courts to address war crimes and crimes against humanity is one approach being pursued.

V. Gender Equality and Women's Rights: African countries are focusing on advancing gender equality and women's rights. Strategies include enacting laws to combat gender-based violence, promoting women's participation in decision-making processes, and implementing policies to ensure equal access to education and healthcare.

VI. Child Rights Protection: Efforts to protect the rights of children are being strengthened through measures such as the enactment of child protection laws, initiatives to combat child labor and trafficking, and programs to provide education and healthcare for vulnerable children.

VII. Human Rights Education and Awareness: Raising awareness about human rights and promoting human rights education is critical to building a culture of respect for human rights. Governments, civil society, and international organizations are working together to integrate human rights education into school curricula and public awareness campaigns.

VIII. Civil Society Engagement: Civil society organizations play a crucial role in advocating for human rights, monitoring human rights violations, and providing support to victims. Governments are encouraged to create an enabling environment for civil society to operate freely and contribute to human rights protection.

IX. International Cooperation: International partners, including the United Nations and other regional organizations, provide support to African countries in their efforts to strengthen human rights protection. Technical assistance, capacity building, and financial support are provided to advance human rights agendas.

X. Inclusive and Participatory Processes: Inclusion and participation are emphasized in efforts to strengthen human rights protection. Engaging with marginalized and vulnerable groups ensures that their rights and perspectives are taken into account in policy-making and implementation.

Hope for a future of empowered humanity through continued human rights advocacy

Hope for a future of empowered humanity through continued human rights advocacy remains strong. Human rights advocacy plays a crucial role in promoting social justice, equality, and dignity for all individuals, regardless of their background or circumstances. Here are some reasons for hope:

I. Global Awareness and Solidarity: Human rights issues are increasingly gaining global attention, thanks to the efforts of human rights advocates, activists, and organizations. In today's interconnected world, people are more aware of human rights violations, and solidarity among individuals and nations is growing stronger.

II. Youth Engagement: Young people are actively engaged in human rights advocacy, demonstrating their passion for social change and their commitment to building a more just and inclusive world. Youth-led movements are driving meaningful conversations and demanding accountability from governments and institutions.

III. Advancements in Technology: Technology has empowered human rights advocates to raise awareness, share information, and mobilize support more effectively. Social media platforms, online campaigns, and digital tools have become essential in amplifying human rights messages and organizing grassroots movements.

IV. Legal Progress: Many countries have made significant legal advancements to protect human rights and hold perpetrators of human rights abuses accountable. National courts, international tribunals, and mechanisms like the International Criminal Court (ICC) contribute to fostering a culture of accountability.

V. Strengthening Regional Bodies: Regional human rights bodies, like the African Commission on Human and Peoples' Rights and the Inter-American Court of Human Rights, continue to play critical roles in advancing human rights protections within their respective regions.

VI. Corporate Social Responsibility: The private sector is increasingly recognizing its role in respecting human rights and contributing to sustainable development. Many companies are adopting human rights policies and practices that uphold labor rights, environmental protections, and ethical business conduct.

VII. Inclusive Policies: Some governments are taking steps to create more inclusive policies that address systemic discrimination and protect vulnerable populations. Efforts to promote gender equality, LGBTQ+ rights, and the rights of persons with disabilities are gaining momentum.

VIII. International Cooperation: Collaborative efforts among nations, regional organizations, and international bodies are fostering collective action to address global human rights challenges. Dialogue and cooperation are essential in finding solutions to cross-border issues.

IX. Resilience of Civil Society: Despite facing challenges and risks, civil society organizations continue to play a vital role in monitoring human rights, providing support to victims, and advocating for change. Their resilience and determination are instrumental in driving progress.

Universal Declaration of Human Rights: The Universal Declaration of Human Rights, adopted by the United Nations in 1948, remains a powerful and universally recognized framework for promoting human rights and guiding advocacy efforts worldwide. While significant challenges persist, the dedication of human rights advocates and the recognition of human rights as fundamental to human dignity offer hope for a future where all individuals can live with dignity, freedom, and equality. Continued human rights advocacy will be crucial in shaping a world where human rights are respected, protected, and fulfilled for every person, regardless of their background or identity.

CHAPTER TWELVE

Conclusion

In conclusion, human rights advocacy stands as a beacon of hope for a future of empowered humanity. Despite the persistent challenges and violations, the unwavering commitment of human rights advocates, activists, and organizations has sparked positive change across the globe. Efforts to strengthen human rights protection in Africa and other regions have gained momentum, leading to increased awareness, solidarity, and legal progress. The engagement of young people, supported by advancements in technology, has breathed new life into the fight for social justice and equality.

The rise of regional human rights bodies and inclusive policies reflects a growing recognition of the importance of respecting the rights of all individuals, irrespective of their background or circumstances. Corporations, too, are embracing social responsibility, contributing to sustainable development and ethical practices. International cooperation, guided by the Universal Declaration of Human Rights, is fostering collective action to address global challenges. The resilience of civil society and its tireless advocacy are driving progress, empowering marginalized communities, and supporting victims of human rights abuses. While there is still much work to be done, the hope for a brighter future lies in the continued commitment to human rights advocacy. As we move forward, let us carry this hope with us, striving to build a world where human rights are not just an aspiration but a reality for all. Through continued advocacy and unwavering dedication, we can create a future where empowered humanity thrives, and human rights are cherished as the foundation of a just and compassionate world.

Summary of key findings and insights

Key Findings and Insights

The Universal Declaration of Human Rights (UDHR) has had a significant impact on human rights in Africa, serving as a benchmark and influencing the development of customary

International law in the region. Many African countries have ratified human rights treaties that amplify the principles of the UDHR, and some have incorporated its provisions into their domestic constitutions and laws.

The African Charter on Human and Peoples' Rights, as well as regional and sub-regional legal instruments, refer to and uphold the principles of the UDHR. The UDHR has been invoked in legal cases, providing a basis for addressing human rights violations and seeking justice for victims.

The impact of the UDHR is not limited to legal frameworks; it has also contributed to shaping societal norms and values regarding human rights in Africa. The struggle to protect and promote human rights in Africa continues, with ongoing efforts to address systemic challenges, such as corruption, poverty, conflict, and discrimination.

International organizations, civil society, and individuals play a crucial role in advocating for human rights, fostering solidarity, and holding perpetrators accountable.

The Russo-Ukrainian War and the Russian invasion of Ukraine have highlighted the importance of international human rights law and accountability mechanisms in addressing war crimes and violations.

The situation in Ukraine underscores the need for continued efforts to strengthen human rights protection globally and the importance of international cooperation and regional bodies in addressing human rights violations.

The future of empowered humanity relies on sustained human rights advocacy, the engagement of young people, corporate social responsibility, and the commitment to uphold human rights principles at all levels of society.

Despite challenges and setbacks, hope for a better future lies in the collective efforts of human rights advocates and the universal aspiration to live in a world where human rights are universally respected and protected.

Hope for a future of empowered humanity through continued human rights advocacy

The hope for a future of empowered humanity lies in the continued and unwavering commitment to human rights advocacy. Human rights advocacy has proven to be a powerful force for positive change, and it holds the potential to create a world where every individual can live with dignity, equality, and freedom.

I. Progressive Change: Human rights advocacy has already achieved significant progress in many parts of the world. Through persistent efforts, discriminatory laws have been repealed, marginalized communities have gained visibility, and access to education and healthcare has improved for millions.

II. Global Solidarity: Human rights issues transcend borders, and advocacy efforts often garner global support. The interconnectedness of our world allows for international cooperation and collective action in addressing human rights challenges.

III. Youth Engagement: Young people around the world are increasingly engaged in human rights activism. Their passion, energy, and fresh perspectives bring new hope and creativity to the movement, ensuring its continuity and effectiveness.

IV. Accountability Mechanisms: International bodies, such as the International Criminal Court (ICC) and regional human rights courts, play a vital role in holding perpetrators of human rights violations accountable. This strengthens the rule of law and deterrence against future abuses.

V. Media and Technology: Advances in media and technology have amplified human rights messages and enabled advocacy to reach a wider audience. Social media platforms provide a powerful tool for mobilizing support and raising awareness.

VI. Corporate Responsibility: More businesses and corporations are recognizing the importance of respecting human rights in their operations and supply chains. Corporate social responsibility efforts can influence positive change and set standards for ethical practices.

VII. Inclusivity and Intersectionality: Human rights advocacy has evolved to embrace the principles of inclusivity and intersectionality, acknowledging that human rights are interconnected and indivisible. This approach fosters a more comprehensive and effective response to human rights challenges.

VIII. Humanitarian Aid and Assistance: Human rights advocacy goes hand in hand with humanitarian aid and assistance. In times of crisis, organizations and individuals come together to provide support and relief to vulnerable populations.

IX. Public Awareness and Education: As more people become aware of human rights issues, they become active participants in advocating for change. Education on human rights is a catalyst for fostering empathy and understanding.

X. Resilience and Perseverance: Throughout history, human rights advocates have faced immense challenges, but their resilience and perseverance have driven progress. The unwavering commitment of human rights defenders continues to inspire hope.

While the road to realizing full human rights protection may be long and challenging, the hope lies in the collective determination of individuals, communities, governments, and organizations to stand up for justice and equality.

By embracing human rights advocacy as a shared responsibility, we can build a future where every person's rights are upheld, and every individual is empowered to live a life of dignity and opportunity.

REFERENCES

Abdulcadir, J., Margairaz, C., Boulvain, M., & Irion, O. (2011, January 6). Care of women with female genital mutilation/cutting. *Swiss Medical Weekly*, 140, w13137. doi:10.4414/smw.2011.13137

Alamy. (1941). German Junkers Ju-87 [Photograph]. Retrieved from Stock Photo – Alamy.

AU UN IST PHOTO / David Mutua. (2014, January 25). FGM awareness session run by the African Union Mission to Somalia at the Walalah Biylooley refugee camp, Mogadishu [Photograph].

Beitz, C. R. (2009). The idea of human rights. Oxford: Oxford University Press. ISBN 978-0-19-957245-8.

Ben-Horin, 1943, p. 169; Taylor 1979, p. 124; Yisreelit, Hevrah Mizrahit (1965). Asian and African Studies, p. 191.

BETTS, R. F. (2012). Decolonization. In ELS BOGAERTS & REMCO RABEN (Eds.), Decolonization: A brief history of the word. Beyond Empire and Nation. The Decolonization of African and Asian societies, 1930s-1970s (pp. 23–38). Brill.

Bryan, D. (April 8, 2012). The Northwest Ordinance of 1787 and its Effects. American HistoryUSA. Retrieved February 23, 2023.

Burns H. Weston, "human rights," Encyclopædia Britannica, 20 March 2014. Archived 18 May 2015 at the Wayback Machine. Retrieved 14 August 2014.

Chomsky, N. (1993). Years 5001: The Conquest Continues. Boston: South End Press.

Christofferson, T. R., & Christofferson, M. S. (2006). France During World War II: From Defeat to Liberation. New York: Fordham University Press. ISBN 978-0-8232-2562- 0.

Clark, C. (2013). The Sleepwalkers: How Europe Went to War in 1914. HarperCollins. ISBN 978-0-06-219922-5.

Clark, N., & Worger, W. (2016). South Africa: The Rise and Fall of Apartheid. New York: Routledge. doi:10.4324/9781315621562. ISBN 978-1-315-62156-2.

Cole, C. M. (2010). Performing South Africa's Truth Commission: Stages of Transition. Indiana University Press. p. 31. ISBN 9780253353900.

Danziger, D., & Gillingham, J. (2004). 1215: The Year of Magna Carta. Hodder Paperbacks. ISBN 978-0340824757.

D'Amato, A. (2009). The Coerciveness of International Law. German Yearbook of International Law, 52, 437-443.

Deng, F. M. (1997). Ethnicity an African predicament. Brookings. Retrieved from https://www.brookings.edu/articles/ethnicity-an-african-predicament/ (accessed: 08.01.2020).

Du Pre, R. H. (1994). Separate but Unequal – The 'Coloured' People of South Africa – A Political History. Jonathan Ball Publishers, Johannesburg, pp. 134–139.

Evans, I. (1997). Bureaucracy and Race: Native Administration in South Africa. Berkeley: U of California.

Ferris, J., & Mawdsley, E. (2015). The Cambridge History of the Second World War, Volume I: Fighting the War. Cambridge: Cambridge University Press.

Fremont-Barnes, G. (2007). Encyclopedia of the Age of Political Revolutions and New Ideologies, 1760–1815. Greenwood. ISBN 978-0-313-04951-4.

Ghuhl, W. (2007). Imperial Japan's World War Two. Transaction Publishers, pp. 7, 30.

Gish, S. (2000). Alfred B. Xuma: African, American, South African. New York University Press, p. 8.

Hett, B. C. (1996). "Goak here": A.J.P. Taylor and 'The Origins of the Second World War.'Canadian Journal of History, 31(2), 315–336.

Hodgkinson, D., & Melchiorre, L. (n.d.). Africa's student movements: history sheds light on modern activism. The Conversation. Retrieved 15 October 2019.

James Nickel, with assistance from Thomas Pogge, M.B.E. Smith, and Leif Wenar, (2005). "Human Rights," Stanford Encyclopedia of Philosophy.

J. Vansina, (1962). A Comparison of African Kingdoms. Africa: Journal of the International African Institute, pp. 324–335.

Kopstein, K. (2000). Comparative Politics: Interests, Identities, and Institutions in a Changing Global Order. Cambridge UP, p. 72. ISBN 9780521633567.

Lonsdale, J. (1985). The European Scramble and Conquest in African History. In The Cambridge History of Africa, from 1870 to 1905, J.D. and R. Oliver (Eds.), Cambridge: Cambridge University Press: 6:680-766.

Maltby, W. S. (1993). Imperialism and Science: Social Impact and Interaction. ABC-CLIO. ISBN 9780313274976.

Mann, G. (1988). The Coming of War: An Account of the Remarkable Events Leading to the Second World War. London: Secker & Warburg.

Mann, G. (2004). The History of Germany Since 1789. London: Penguin.

Marivate, P. B. (1943). The Bantu: Past and Present: An Ethnographical and Historical Study of the Native Races of South Africa. Lovedale Press. Lovedale, South Africa.

Michael Crowder, (1968). West Africa Under Colonial Rule. London: Hutchinson & Co., 1968, pp. 419–421.

Nabobo-Baba, U. (2006). Knowing and Learning: An Indigenous Fijian Approach. Institute of Pacific Studies, University of the South Pacific, pp. 1–3, 37–40. ISBN 978-9820203792.

Naicker, V. (2023). The problem of epistemological critique in contemporary Decolonial theory. Social Dynamics, 1–22. doi:10.1080/02533952.2023.2226497.

Njock, L. C. (2016). Human Rights in Africa: A Comparative Study of the African Human and People's Rights Charter and the New Tanzanian Bill of Rights. Intersentia. ISBN 978-1-78068-339-3.

Ocheni, S., & Nwankwo, B. C. (2012). Analysis of Colonialism and Its Impact in Africa. Journal of Cross-Cultural Communication (CSCanada), 8(3), 46-54.

Okeowo, A. (2017). A Moonless, Starless Sky: Ordinary Women and Men Fighting Extremism in Africa. Hachette. ISBN 9780316382932.

Patterson, O. (1995). Freedom, Slavery, and the Modern construction of Rights in Hufton (Ed.), Historical Change and Human Rights: The Oxford Amnesty Lectures 1994, New York: Basic Books, p. 176.

Peter Crooks (July 2015). Exporting Magna Carta: Exclusionary liberties in Ireland and the world. History Ireland, 23(4).

Peter Turchin, Jonathan M. Adams, and Thomas D. Hall, (2006). East-West Orientation of Historical Empires and Modern States, Journal of World-Systems Research, Vol. XII, No. II.

Price, M. E. (1993). National Socialism and the Religion of Nature. New York: Routledge. ISBN 978-0-415-07531-7.

Prost, A. (1977). Origins and Consequences of the French Section of the Workers' International (SFIO), 1905–1914. French Historical Studies, 10(4), 580–599.

R Strayer, R. (2001). Decolonization, Democratization, and Communist Reform: The Soviet Collapse in Comparative Perspective. Journal of World History, 12(2), 375– 406.

Rapley, J. (2007). Twentieth-Century South Africa. Macmillan, p. 48. ISBN 978-1-4039- 4733-5.

Reynolds, D. (1994). The Creation of the Anglo-American Alliance, 1937–1941: A Study on Competitive Cooperation. Chapel Hill, NC: University of North Carolina Press. ISBN 978-0-8078-4494-4.

Robinson, G. T. F. (1926). African Parallels: A Comparison of Political and Social Development in British Africa with French and Belgian Africa. Cambridge: Cambridge University Press.

Roy, A. J. (2001). Sovereignty and Decolonization: Realizing Indigenous Self- Determination at the United Nations and in Canada (Thesis). University of Victoria.

Schwoerer, L. G. (1990). Locke, Lockean Ideas, and the Glorious Revolution. Journal of the History of Ideas, 51(4), 531–548.

Sen, A. (2005). The Argumentative Indian: Writings on Indian History, Culture and Identity. Picador. ISBN 978-0-312-42564-3.

Shell, M. (2015). Island of Shame: The Secret History of the U.S. Military Base on Diego Garcia. New York: Princeton University Press. ISBN 978-0-691-16185-8.

Shenton, R., & Shenton, S. (1983). The Physical Geography of Africa. Oxford University Press. ISBN 978-0-19-874067-7.

Smith, S., & Jeal, T. (2007). Mau Mau 1952–1960: The Kenyan Emergency. Osprey Publishing. ISBN 978-1-84603-096-7.

St, International Labour. (n.d.). Labour standards. www.ilo.org. Retrieved 27 April 2020.

Steger, M. B. (2005). Judicial Review in International Perspective. In The Judicialization of Politics in Latin America, edited by Rachel Sieder, Line Schjolden, and Alan Angell (pp. 281–298). Palgrave Macmillan. ISBN 978-1-4039-6333-5.

Stephen Baier (1998). The Impact of the Second World War on Canadian Economic Development. The Canadian Historical Review, 79(2), 207–240.

Strohm, P. (1976). Afonso de Albuquerque: First Governor of Portuguese India. Hamden, CT: Archon Books.

Thomas, M. (2003). Empire and History Writing in Britain c. 1750–2012. Manchester: Manchester University Press. ISBN 978-0-7190-6726-7.

Thompson, L. (2001). A History of South Africa. New Haven, CT: Yale University Press. ISBN 978-0-300-08762-3.

Tomasevich, J. (2001). War and Revolution in Yugoslavia, 1941–1945: Occupation and Collaboration. Stanford: Stanford University Press. ISBN 978-0-8047-3615-2.

Van Hartesveldt, F. R. (2004). The Korean War: Essential Histories. Osprey Publishing. ISBN 978-1- 84603-079-0.

Van Ypersele, L. (2014). Histoire de la Belgique pour tous. Bruxelles: Éditions Racine.

Weller, M. (2009). Universal human rights: a comparative research of the constitutions of human rights and the rights of man. Springer. ISBN 978-3-540-89091-1.

White, J. F. (2003). The highest stage of white supremacy: the origins of segregation in South Africa and the American South. Cambridge; New York: Cambridge University Press. ISBN 978-0-521-80480-8.

Wilson, J. F. (n.d.). Brief history of Rhodesia/Zimbabwe. The Zimbabwe Situation. The Heritage Portal. Retrieved 7 June 2020.

Wright, A. D. (1986). The Dissolution of the Austro-Hungarian Empire, 1867–1918. Longman Group Ltd. ISBN 978-0-582-48365-3.

Wylie, N. (2002). Dissenting Voices: Rediscovering the Irish Progressive Presbyterian Tradition. Ulster Historical Foundation. ISBN 978-1-903688-09-8.

Zaloga, S. (2011). The Devil's Garden: Rommel's Desperate Defense of Omaha Beach on D-Day. Stackpole Books. ISBN 978-0-8117-0794-5.

www.ingramcontent.com/pod-product-compliance
Lightning Source LLC
Chambersburg PA
CBHW060041260726

48658CB00004B/1135